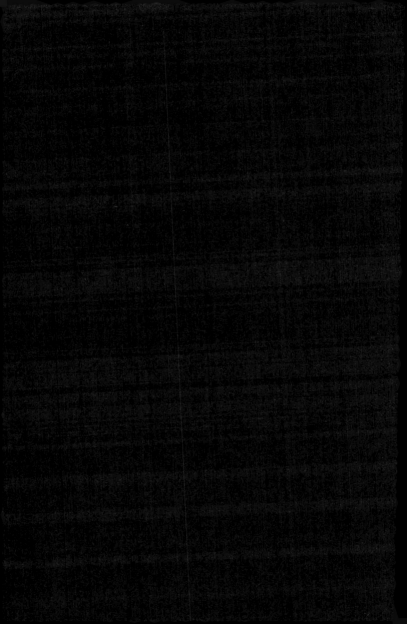

HOW TO BE A FRIEND

ANCIENT WISDOM FOR MODERN READERS

Ancient Wisdom for Modern Readers presents the timeless
and timely ideas of classical thinkers in lively new translations. Enlightening
and entertaining, these books make the practical wisdom of the ancient
world accessible for modern life.

■ ■ ■ ■

How to Die: An Ancient Guide to the
End of Life by Seneca.
Edited, translated, and introduced by James S. Romm

How to Win an Argument: An Ancient Guide to the Art
of Persuasion by Marcus Tullius Cicero.
Selected, edited, and translated by James M. May

How to Grow Old: Ancient Wisdom for the Second Half of
Life by Marcus Tullius Cicero.
Translated and with an introduction by Philip Freeman

How to Run a Country: An Ancient Guide for Modern
Leaders by Marcus Tullius Cicero.
Selected, translated, and with an introduction by Philip Freeman

How to Win an Election: An Ancient Guide for Modern
Politicians by Quintus Tullius Cicero.
Translated and with an introduction by Philip Freeman

HOW TO BE A FRIEND

■ ■ ■ ■ ■

An Ancient Guide to True Friendship

Marcus Tullius Cicero

Translated and with an introduction by
Philip Freeman

PRINCETON UNIVERSITY PRESS

PRINCETON AND OXFORD

Requests for permission to reproduce material from this work
should be sent to
Permissions, Princeton University Press

Published by Princeton University Press,
41 William Street, Princeton, New Jersey 08540

In the United Kingdom: Princeton University Press,
6 Oxford Street, Woodstock, Oxfordshire OX20 1TR

press.princeton.edu

Jacket image: © Lestoquoy Véronique / Dreamstime

ISBN 978-0-691-17719-9

Library of Congress Control Number: 2017963962

British Library Cataloging-in-Publication Data is available

This book has been composed in
Stempel Garamond LT Std and Futura

Printed on acid-free paper. ∞

Printed in the United States of America

1 3 5 7 9 10 8 6 4 2

CONTENTS

INTRODUCTION

The best friend of Marcus Tullius Cicero was named Atticus.

His real name was Titus Pomponius, but he took the name Atticus because of his love for Greece, especially the city of Athens in the region of Attica, where he spent many years of his adult life. He and Cicero became fast friends as young men and remained so throughout their long lives. Cicero was devoted to Roman politics and spent most of his years in that turbulent city during the first century BC, a time of tremendous upheaval and civil war. Atticus, on the other hand, watched Roman politics from the safe distance of Athens while remaining in close contact with the leading men of both sides

back in Rome. Even though they were often apart, Cicero and Atticus exchanged letters over the years that reveal a friendship of rare devotion and warm affection.

In the year 44 BC, Cicero was in his sixties—an old man by Roman standards—living on his farm outside of Rome removed from political power by the dictatorship of Julius Caesar. He turned to writing to ease the pain of exile and the recent loss of his beloved daughter. In a period of months, he produced some of the most readable and influential essays ever written on subjects ranging from the nature of the gods and the proper role of government to the joys of growing older and the secret to finding happiness in life. Among these works was a short essay on friendship dedicated to Atticus.

How to Be a Friend—or in Latin *De Amicitia*—is arguably the best book ever written on the

subject. The heartfelt advice it gives is honest and moving in a way few works of ancient times are. Some Romans had viewed friendship in mostly practical terms as a relationship between people for mutual advantage. Cicero doesn't deny that such friendships are important, but he reaches beyond the utilitarian to praise a deeper kind of friendship in which two people find in each other another self who doesn't seek profit or advantage from the other person.

Greek philosophers such as Plato and Aristotle had written about friendship hundreds of years earlier. Indeed Cicero was deeply influenced by their writings. But Cicero goes beyond his predecessors and creates in this short work a compelling guide to finding, keeping, and appreciating those people in our lives we value not for what they can give us, but because we find in them a kindred soul.

INTRODUCTION

The fictional setting of the book is a discussion that took place in a garden many years earlier in 129 BC between an aged Roman general and orator named Gaius Laelius and his two younger sons-in-law, Gaius Fannius and Quintus Mucius Scaevola. Laelius was in mourning, having lost his best friend Scipio Africanus just a few days earlier. The two younger men plead with Laelius to tell them what he and Scipio learned about true friendship over their lifetime together — which, after some preliminary protest, the older man does. Cicero says that Scaevola in turn revealed to him decades later what he learned that day. Cicero was a young man at that time studying at the feet of Scaevola, who was by then an elder statesman and distinguished lawyer. Cicero then records for his friend Atticus and all his readers through the centuries the words of Laelius — in truth the words of Cicero — on the nature of friendship.

INTRODUCTION

How to Be a Friend is filled with timeless advice on friendship. Among the best is:

1. *There are different kinds of friendships*: Cicero acknowledges that there are many good people we come in contact with in our lives we call our friends, be they business associates, neighbors, or any manner of acquaintances. But he makes a key distinction between these common and quite useful friendships and those rare friends we bind ourselves to on a much deeper level. These special friendships are necessarily rare, because they require so much time and investment of ourselves. But these are the friends that deeply change our lives, just as we change theirs.

2. *Only good people can be true friends*: People of poor moral character can have friends, but they can only be friends of utility for the simple reason that real friendship requires trust,

wisdom, and basic goodness. Tyrants and scoundrels can use each other, just as they can use good people, but bad people can never find real friendship in life.

3. *We should choose our friends with care*: We have to be deliberate about forming our friendships if for no other reason than that they can be very messy and painful to end if we find out the friend was not the person we thought. We should take our time, move slowly, and discover what lies deep in a person's heart before we make the investment of self that true friendship requires.

4. *Friends make you a better person*: No one can thrive in isolation. Left on our own, we will stagnate and become unable to see ourselves as we are. A true friend will challenge you to become better because he appreciates the potential inside you.

5. *Make new friends, but keep the old*: No one is a sweeter friend than someone who has been with you from the beginning. But don't limit yourself to the companions of youth, whose friendship may have been based on interests you no longer share. Always be open to new friendships, including those with younger people. Both you and they will be the richer for it.

6. *Friends are honest with each other*: Friends will always tell you what you need to hear, not what you want them to say. There are plenty of people in the world who will flatter you for their own purposes, but only a real friend—or an enemy—will risk your anger by telling you the truth. And being a good person yourself, you should listen to your friends and welcome what they have to say.

7. *The reward of friendship is friendship itself*: Cicero acknowledges that there are practical

advantages to friendship—advice, companionship, support in difficult times—but at its heart true friendship is not a business relationship. It doesn't seek repayment, and it doesn't keep score.

8. *A friend never asks another friend to do something wrong*: A friend will risk much for another, but not honor. If a friend asks you to lie, cheat, or do something shameful, consider carefully if that person is who you really thought he was. Since friendship is based on goodness, it cannot exist when evil is expected of it.

9. *Friendships can change over time*: Friendships from youth will not be the same in old age—nor should they be. Life changes all of us with time, but the core values and qualities that drew us to friends in years past can survive the test of time. And like fine wine, the best of friendships will improve with age.

10. *Without friends, life is not worth living*: Or as Cicero says: "Suppose a god carried you far away to a place where you were granted an abundance of every material good nature could wish for, but denied the possibility of ever seeing a human being. Wouldn't you have to be as hard as iron to endure that sort of life? Wouldn't you, utterly alone, lose every capacity for joy and pleasure?"

Cicero's little book on friendship had a tremendous influence on writers in the ages following him, from St. Augustine to the Italian poet Dante and beyond, and was one of the earliest books translated into and printed in English. It is no less valuable today. In a modern age of technology and a relentless focus on the self that threatens the very idea of deep and lasting friendships, Cicero has more to say to us than ever.

HOW TO BE A FRIEND

Laelius de Amicitia

1. Quintus Mucius augur multa narrare de Gaio Laelio socero suo memoriter et iucunde solebat, nec dubitare illum in omni sermone appellare sapientem. Ego autem a patre ita eram deductus ad Scaevolam sumpta virili toga, ut, quoad possem et liceret, a senis latere numquam discederem. Itaque multa ab eo prudenter disputata, multa etiam breviter et commode dicta memoriae mandabam, fierique studebam eius prudentia doctior. Quo mortuo me ad pontificem Scaevolam contuli, quem unum nostrae civitatis et ingenio et iustitia praestantissimum audeo dicere. Sed de hoc alias; nunc redeo ad augurem.

How to Be a Friend

1. Quintus Mucius Scaevola[1] the augur[2] used to tell stories happily from his memory about his father-in-law Gaius Laelius,[3] a man he never hesitated to call by his nickname "the Wise." When I put on the toga of manhood,[4] my father brought me to Scaevola so that, as far as I was able and allowed, I would stay by the old man's side. I was eager to profit from his good judgment, so I made a point of memorizing many of his learned discussions as well as his short, useful sayings. After he died, I attached myself to his cousin Scaevola[5] the pontifex,[6] who, I dare say, had more integrity and ability than any man in Rome. But I shall speak of him another time. For now I want to return to Scaevola the augur.

2. Cum saepe multa, tum memini domi in hemicyclio sedentem, ut solebat, cum et ego essem una et pauci admodum familiares, in eum sermonem illum incidere, qui tum fere multis erat in ore. Meministi enim profecto, Attice, et eo magis, quod Publio Sulpicio utebare multum, cum is tribunus plebis capitali odio a Quinto Pompeio qui tum erat consul dissideret, quocum coniunctissime et amantissime vixerat, quanta esset hominum vel admiratio vel querela.

3. Itaque tum Scaevola, cum in eam ipsam mentionem incidisset, exposuit nobis sermonem Laeli de amicitia, habitum ab illo secum et cum altero genero Gaio Fannio Marci filio,

2. Although I remember many things he said, one particular conversation stands out in my mind. He was sitting at home that day on his semicircular garden bench as he often did. I was there along with just a few of his closest friends when he took up a topic that was on everyone's lips.

Atticus,[7] you were very friendly with Publius Sulpicius[8] in those days, and I'm sure you remember well how he separated himself in hatred from Quintus Pompeius when he was tribune of the plebs[9] and Pompeius was consul,[10] even though he and Pompeius had been the closest and dearest of friends. Everyone marveled at their admiration for each other, followed by their bitter recriminations.

3. While we were sitting there discussing this situation, Scaevola told us of a conversation he had once had with Laelius concerning friendship. He said Laelius' other son-in-law Gaius

paucis diebus post mortem Africani. Eius disputationis sententias memoriae mandavi, quas hoc libro exposui arbitratu meo; quasi enim ipsos induxi loquentes, ne 'inquam' et 'inquit' saepius interponeretur, atque ut tamquam a praesentibus coram haberi sermo videretur.

4. Cum enim saepe mecum ageres, ut de amicitia scriberem aliquid, digna mihi res cum omnium cognitione tum nostra familiaritate visa est; itaque feci non invitus, ut prodessem multis rogatu tuo. Sed ut in Catone Maiore, qui est scriptus ad te de senectute, Catonem induxi senem disputantem, quia nulla videbatur aptior persona quae de illa aetate loqueretur quam eius qui et diutissime senex fuerit, et in ipsa senectute praeter ceteros floruisset; sic cum

Fannius,[11] the son of Marcus, had also been there and that the discussion had taken place a few days after the death of Africanus.[12] I committed to memory the main points of that discussion and have set them forth in this book in my own way. I've put the whole conversation into direct speech to avoid constantly repeating "I said" or "he said," and so that the discussion seems to be taking place before our eyes with the speakers present.

4. You have often encouraged me, Atticus, to write something for you about friendship. And I believe it's a subject worthy of everyone's consideration, but also quite well-suited to our own relationship as friends. Therefore I am quite willing to take on this topic for the general good at your urging. I've adopted the same style as in my *Cato the Elder* which I wrote to you on the subject of old age.[13] In that work, I gave Cato as a very old man the principal role

accepissemus a patribus maxime memorabilem Gai Laeli et Publi Scipionis familiaritatem fuisse, idonea mihi Laeli persona visa est quae de amicitia ea ipsa dissereret quae disputata ab eo meminisset Scaevola. Genus autem hoc sermonum positum in hominum veterum auctoritate et eorum illustrium, plus nescioquo pacto videtur habere gravitatis; itaque ipse mea legens sic afficior interdum ut Catonem, non me loqui existimem.

5. Sed ut tum ad senem senex de senectute, sic hoc libro ad amicum amicissimus scripsi de amicitia; tum est Cato locutus quo erat nemo fere senior temporibus illis, nemo prudentior;

since it seemed appropriate to have someone as speaker who had been elderly a long time and had prospered more than most men. Since we have learned from our ancestors that a most memorable friendship existed between Gaius Laelius and Publius Scipio, it therefore seemed appropriate that Laelius be the one in my story to pass on the ideas about friendship that Scaevola said he remembered him saying. I don't know why, but it seems more dignified and authoritative to have discussions like this put into the mouths of men from the past, especially those of good reputation. I confess that when I read my own work on old age, sometimes I'm so moved that I think it's actually Cato speaking and not myself.

5. In that book I wrote as an old man to an old man on old age; now in this book I have written as a dear friend to a friend about friendship. In that book Cato was the speaker, for

nunc Laelius et sapiens (sic enim est habitus) et
amicitiae gloria excellens de amicitia loquetur.
Tu velim a me animum parumper avertas, Lae-
lium loqui ipsum putes. Gaeus Fannius et Quin-
tus Mucius ad socerum veniunt post mortem
Africani; ab his sermo oritur, respondet Lae-
lius, cuius tota disputatio est de amicitia; quam
legens te ipse cognosces.

6. Fannius: Sunt ista, Laeli; nec enim melior
vir fuit Africano quisquam nec clarior. Sed ex-
istimare debes omnium oculos in te esse coniec-
tos: unum te sapientem et appellant et existi-
mant. Tribuebatur hoc modo M. Catoni, scimus
L. Acilium apud patres nostros appellatum
esse sapientem, sed uterque alio quodam modo:

scarcely anyone in his day was older and none wiser. In this book Laelius speaks concerning friendship, since he was wise—as everyone says—and surpassing all in his reputation as a friend. So for a little while I'd like you to pay no attention to me as the author, but think Laelius himself is speaking to you. Gaius Fannius and Quintus Mucius Scaevola have come to their father-in-law's house just after the death of Africanus. They begin the conversation, then Laelius responds and devotes the whole discussion to friendship. When you read it, you will recognize yourself.

6. *Fannius*: What you say is true, Laelius. There was never a better or more distinguished man than Africanus. But you ought to realize that the eyes of all men are now fixed on you. You're the one they call wise—and they believe it too. People not so long ago thought the same of Marcus Cato, while our ancestors gave that

Acilius quia prudens esse in iure civili putaba-
tur, Cato quia multarum rerum usum habebat.
Multa eius et in senatu et in foro vel provisa
prudenter vel acta constanter vel responsa acute
ferebantur; propterea quasi cognomen iam
habebat in senectute sapientis.

7. Te autem alio quodam modo, non solum
natura et moribus, verum etiam studio et doc-
trina esse sapientem: nec sicut vulgus, sed ut
eruditi solent appellare sapientem, qualem in
reliqua Graecia neminem (nam qui Septem ap-
pellantur, eos qui ista subtilius quaerunt in nu-
mero sapientium non habent), Athenis unum
accepimus, et eum quidem etiam Apollinis ora-
culo sapientissimum iudicatum: hanc esse in te
sapientiam existimant, ut omnia tua in te posita

title to Lucius Acilius, though each was wise in a different way. Acilius was so called because of his skill in civil law, but Cato gained the name for his talents in many areas. They say that many times both in the Senate chamber and in the forum he gave ample evidence of his prudent foresight, his steady resolve, and his shrewd responses in debate. By the end of his days "the Wise" was practically his last name.[14]

7. They say that you, however, are wise in a rather different way, not only in your natural abilities and character, but in your knowledge and desire to learn. They speak of your wisdom not as the common people use the term but as scholars mean it. *This* sort of wisdom we hear belonged to no one in all of Greece—for those who investigate such things with strict precision don't even consider wise those who are called the "Seven Sages"—except one man in Athens,

esse ducas, humanosque casus virtute inferiores putes. Itaque ex me quaerunt, credo ex hoc item Scaevola, quonam pacto mortem Africani feras; eoque magis, quod proximis Nonis, cum in hortos D. Bruti auguris commentandi causa, ut adsolet, venissemus, tu non adfuisti, qui diligentissime semper illum diem et illud munus solitus esses obire.

8. Scaevola: Quaerunt quidem, Gai Laeli, multi, ut est a Fannio dictum. Sed ego id respondeo quod animum adverti, te dolorem quem

who was judged to be most wise by the oracle of Apollo himself.[15]

But men consider you to have such great wisdom that you believe that all your treasures dwell within you and that you believe the rise or fall of fortune in human life matters much less than doing what is right.

So people have been asking me, just as I believe they are asking Scaevola here, how you are bearing the death of your friend Africanus. The inquiries have become more frequent since you did not join us last month on the Nones at the country house of Decimus Brutus when we had our customary meeting of the augurs. Everyone noticed you weren't there even though you have always been faithful in your attendance and in all your duties as an augur.[16]

8. *Scaevola*: Many people are asking about you, Gaeus Laelius, just as Fannius has said. But I tell them what I have seen with my own

acceperis cum summi viri tum amicissimi morte, ferre moderate; nec potuisse non commoveri, nec fuisse id humanitatis tuae. Quod autem Nonis in collegio nostro non adfuisses, valetudinem respondeo causae, non maestitiam fuisse.

Laelius: Recte tu quidem, Scaevola, et vere. Nec enim ab isto officio, quod semper usurpavi cum valerem, abduci incommodo meo debui, nec ullo casu arbitror hoc constanti homini posse contingere, ut ulla intermissio fiat officii.

9. Tu autem, Fanni, quod mihi tantum tribui dicis quantum ego nec adgnosco nec postulo, facis amice, sed ut mihi videris, non recte iudicas de Catone. Aut enim nemo, quod quidem magis credo, aut si quisquam, ille sapiens fuit. Quomodo, ut alia omittam, mortem filii tulit!

eyes, that you are bearing the pain of losing your dearest friend, who was a very great man, with composure. Of course you are deeply affected by his death, as any man as caring as you would be, but I let them know you were absent from our gathering of augurs on the Nones because of illness, not grief.

Laelius: You are quite right, Scaevola, and what you told them is true. I have always carried out my duties except when illness prevented me. I would never neglect them because of personal inconvenience. No man with any sense of responsibility would allow himself to ignore his duties because of such considerations.

9. Now Fannius, when you tell me that men are paying such compliments to me, you're very kind, but I must say that I didn't ask for such praise, nor can I accept it. As for Cato, I don't think your estimate of him is high enough. For either no man is truly wise—as I am inclined to

Memineram Paulum, videram Galum; sed hi in pueris, Cato in perfecto et spectato viro.

10. Quam ob rem cave Catoni anteponas ne istum quidem ipsum quem Apollo, ut ais, sapientissimum iudicavit; huius enim facta, illius dicta laudantur.

De me autem (ut iam cum utroque vestrum loquar) sic habetote: Ego si Scipionis desiderio me moveri negem, quam id recte faciam viderint sapientes, sed certe mentiar. Moveor enim tali amico orbatus qualis, ut arbitror, nemo umquam erit; ut confirmare possum, nemo certe fuit. Sed non egeo medicina: me ipse consolor, et maxime illo solacio, quod eo errore careo quo amicorum decessu plerique angi solent. Nihil

believe—or if anyone can be called wise, it was Cato. Putting everything else about him to one side, look at how he bore the death of his son. I remember when Paulus suffered a similar loss, and I saw Galus when his son died, but their sons were only boys, whereas Cato's was a young man clearly in the prime of life.[17]

10. So be careful not to put anyone ahead of Cato, not even the man Apollo judged the wisest of all. After all, Cato was praised for his deeds, Socrates for his words.

Now regarding me, let me speak to both of you at once—and please believe what I say is true. If I were to claim that the death of Scipio didn't cause me sorrow, wise men would judge what I say and certainly find that I am lying. For I am deeply moved by the death of a friend such as I will never have again, or I least such as I never had before. But I do have a remedy of sorts. I console myself—and it is a great

mali accidisse Scipioni puto: mihi accidit, si quid accidit. Suis autem incommodis graviter angi non amicum, sed se ipsum amantis est.

11. Cum illo vero quis neget actum esse praeclare? Nisi enim, quod ille minime putabat, immortalitatem optare vellet, quid non adeptus est quod homini fas esset optare? Qui summam spem civium, quam de eo iam puero habuerant, continuo adulescens incredibili virtute superavit; qui consulatum petivit numquam, factus consul est bis, primum ante tempus, iterum sibi suo tempore, rei publicae paene sero; qui duabus urbibus eversis, inimicissimis huic imperio non modo praesentia verum etiam futura bella delevit. Quid dicam de moribus facillimis, de

consolation—that I am spared the delusion that tortures most people face when a dear friend dies. You see, I don't believe that any evil has befallen Scipio. If anyone has suffered a loss, I think it is me. Still, if you let your sorrow overwhelm you, you're not showing how much you loved your friend, only how much you love yourself.

11. Who would deny that life went wonderfully well for Scipio? Unless he was hoping to live forever—which he certainly wasn't—what is there proper for a man to obtain in life that he didn't? When he was still a child his countrymen looked forward to great achievements by him; and even as a young man he surpassed these goals through his great merit. Though he never sought the consulship, he was elected to the office twice—the first time before he was of legal age, the second at the proper time, though almost too late for the Republic. He conquered

pietate in matrem, liberalitate in sorores, boni-
tate in suos, iustitia in omnes? Nota sunt vobis;
quam autem civitati carus fuerit, maerore fu-
neris indicatum est. Quid igitur hunc paucorum
annorum accessio iuvare potuisset? Senectus
enim quamvis non sit gravis, ut memini Cato-
nem anno ante quam est mortuus mecum et
cum Scipione disserere, tamen aufert eam virid-
itatem in qua etiam nunc erat Scipio.

12. Quam ob rem vita quidem talis fuit vel
fortuna vel gloria, ut nihil posset accedere;
moriendi autem sensum celeritas abstulit. Quo
de genere mortis difficile dictu est; quid homi-
nes suspicentur, videtis; hoc vere tamen licet

the two cities which were the gravest threats to our country and thereby did away with present and future wars.[18] And what should I say of his engaging manners, his devotion to his mother, his generosity with his sisters, his kindness to relatives, his fairness to everyone? These things are well known to both of you. The love the whole people had for him was shown by the outpouring of grief at his funeral. What therefore could he have gained by a few more years of life? Although old age doesn't need to be a burden—as Cato maintained a year before his own death in his discussion with Scipio and myself—it does take away that freshness which Scipio kept until the end.

12. On account of this, his life was such that neither fortune nor glory could have added more to it. Beyond this, the suddenness of his death took away any sense of dying. How exactly he died is difficult to say. You both know

dicere, Publio Scipioni, ex multis diebus quos in vita celeberrimos laetissimosque viderit, illum diem clarissimum fuisse, cum senatu dimisso domum reductus ad vesperum est a patribus conscriptis, populo Romano, sociis et Latinis, pridie quam excessit e vita, ut ex tam alto dignitatis gradu ad superos videatur deos potius quam ad inferos pervenisse.

13. Neque enim assentior eis qui haec nuper disserere coeperunt, cum corporibus simul animos interire atque omnia morte deleri. Plus apud me antiquorum auctoritas valet: vel nostrorum maiorum qui mortuis tam religiosa iura tribuerunt, quod non fecissent profecto si nihil ad eos pertinere arbitrarentur; vel eorum qui in hac terra fuerunt, Magnamque Graeciam (quae nunc quidem deleta est, tum florebat) institutis et praeceptis suis erudierunt; vel eius qui Apollinis oraculo sapientissimus est iudicatus, qui

what people suspect.[19] But I will say that of the very many joyous and celebrated days in the life of Scipio, that day before his death was the greatest of all. After the Senate had been dismissed, he was escorted home by the senators, by the Roman people, and by his allies among the people of Italy, so that he seemed to pass from such a lofty status not to the shades below but to the gods above.

13. I don't agree with those who have begun to argue recently that the body and spirit perish together and that death destroys all things. I give more authority to the older views, whether it be those of our ancestors who honored the dead with great reverence—they would not have done so if they thought the dead didn't care—or those who lived nearby in southern Italy, in the region known as Greater Greece, now gone but then flourishing, who by their teachings and principles so enriched us.[20] I also give more

non tum hoc tum illud, ut in plerisque, sed idem semper, animos hominum esse divinos, eisque cum ex corpore excessissent, reditum in caelum patere, optimoque et iustissimo cuique expeditissimum.

14. Quod idem Scipioni videbatur; qui quidem quasi praesagiret, perpaucis ante mortem diebus, cum et Philus et Manilius adessent et alii plures, tuque etiam, Scaevola, mecum venisses, triduum disseruit de re publica, cuius disputationis fuit extremum fere de immortalitate animorum, quae se in quiete per visum ex Africano audisse dicebat. Id si ita est, ut optimi cuiusque animus in morte facillime evolet tamquam e custodia vinclisque corporis, cui censemus cursum ad deos faciliorem fuisse quam Scipioni? Quocirca maerere hoc eius eventu

authority to the man whom the oracle of Apollo declared wisest of men, Socrates, who would argue both sides of almost any subject, but always maintained that human souls were divine. He believed that when the soul left the body, the road back to the heavens lay before it—with the easiest path awaiting souls that were most virtuous and just.

14. Scipio believed this as well. In fact a few days before his death, as if he knew the end was coming, he discussed this with me, Philus, Manilius, and you, Scaevola, who had gone with me, along with many others who were there. For three days he talked about our country, then towards the end of the conversation he turned to the immortality of the soul and revealed what he claimed to have heard in a dream from his uncle Africanus the Elder.[21] If it's true that the souls of the best men most easily escape the bondage and chains of the body after death,

vereor ne invidi magis quam amici sit. Sin autem illa veriora, ut idem interitus sit animorum et corporum, nec ullus sensus maneat, ut nihil boni est in morte, sic certe nihil mali. Sensu enim amisso fit idem quasi natus non esset omnino; quem tamen esse natum et nos gaudemus, et haec civitas dum erit laetabitur.

15. Quam ob rem cum illo quidem, ut supra dixi, actum optime est, mecum incommodius; quem fuerat aequius, ut prius introieram, sic prius exire de vita. Sed tamen recordatione nostrae amicitiae sic fruor ut beate vixisse videar, quia cum Scipione vixerim; quocum mihi coniuncta cura de publica re et de privata fuit, quocum et domus fuit et militia communis, et id in quo est omnis vis amicitiae, voluntatum

who can we imagine had an easier journey to the gods than Scipio? Therefore I fear that grieving at his death would be more of a sign of envy than of friendship. But on the other hand if it's true that the soul and body perish together and no consciousness survives death, then it follows that although there is nothing good in death there is also nothing evil. Because if sensation passes away, it's the same as if we had never been born. But we do rejoice that Scipio was born, as will our country as long as it exists.

15. And so as I've already said, things turned out very well with Scipio, but less so with me. Seeing that I was born before him, it would have been more fair if I had departed life first. But still, I rejoice in remembering our friendship and believe that my life was blessed because I was able to live it with Scipio. We shared together all our public and private cares, we lived together in the same home, soldiered

studiorum sententiarum summa consensio. Itaque non tam ista me sapientiae, quam modo Fannius commemoravit, fama delectat, falsa praesertim, quam quod amicitiae nostrae memoriam spero sempiternam fore; idque eo mihi magis est cordi, quod ex omnibus saeculis vix tria aut quattuor nominantur paria amicorum; quo in genere sperare videor Scipionis et Laeli amicitiam notam posteritati fore.

16. Fannius: Istuc quidem, Laeli, ita necesse est. Sed quoniam amicitiae mentionem fecisti et sumus otiosi, pergratum mihi feceris, spero item Scaevolae, si quem ad modum soles de ceteris rebus quae ex te quaeruntur, sic de amicitia disputaris quid sentias, qualem existimes, quae praecepta des.

together in the same campaigns, and enjoyed the very essence of friendship—a common set of beliefs, aspirations, and opinions. Therefore I take less delight in my reputation for wisdom which Fannius has mentioned, especially since it is undeserved, than in the hope that people will long remember the friendship I shared with Scipio. This aspiration is all the more pleasing to me because in the whole course of history only three or four pairs of true friends are recorded.[22] I hope that the friendship of Scipio and Laelius will be known to future generations as one of these.

16. *Fannius*: Your hope will certainly come true, Laelius. But since you have mentioned friendship and since we are free from public business at the moment, you would please me very much—and Scaevola too, I think—if you would follow your usual custom when questions are put to you and tell us what you

Scaevola: Mihi vero erit gratum, atque id ipsum cum tecum agere conarer, Fannius antevortit. Quam ob rem utrique nostrum gratum admodum feceris.

17. Laelius: Ego vero non gravarer, si mihi ipse confiderem; nam et praeclara res est, et sumus, ut dixit Fannius, otiosi. Sed quis ego sum, aut quae est in me facultas? Doctorum est ista consuetudo eaque Graecorum, ut eis ponatur de quo disputent quamvis subito; magnum opus est egetque exercitatione non parva. Quam ob rem quae disputari de amicitia possunt, ab eis censeo petatis qui ista profitentur: ego vos hortari tantum possum ut amicitiam omnibus rebus humanis anteponatis; nihil est enim tam naturae aptum, tam conveniens ad res vel secundas vel adversas.

believe about friendship, both what you think it is and how we might practice it.

Scaevola: It would be pleasing to me as well. In fact I was about to make the same request of you before Fannius spoke. Both of us would be most grateful to hear what you have to say on the subject.

17. *Laelius*: I'd certainly have no objection if I had any confidence that I could say something worthwhile. For the subject of friendship is a worthy one, and, as Fannius said, we have no pressing business at the moment. But who am I to talk about it, and what talent do I have in such things? The people who are trained at discoursing about something with no preparation are philosophers and Greeks at that. It is a difficult thing to do and requires no small amount of practice. If you truly want someone able to delve deeply into the subject of friendship, I advise you to seek out people who claim

18. Sed hoc primum sentio, nisi in bonis amicitiam esse non posse. Neque id ad vivum reseco, ut illi qui haec subtilius disserunt, fortasse vere, sed ad communem utilitatem parum: negant enim quemquam esse virum bonum nisi sapientem. Sit ita sane; sed eam sapientiam interpretantur, quam adhuc mortalis nemo est consecutus; nos autem ea quae sunt in usu vitaque communi, non ea quae finguntur aut optantur, spectare debemus. Numquam ego dicam C. Fabricium, M'. Curium, Ti. Coruncanium, quos sapientes nostri maiores iudicabant, ad istorum normam fuisse sapientes. Quare sibi habeant sapientiae nomen et invidiosum et obscurum: concedant ut viri boni fuerint. Ne id

to be skilled at such discussions. All I can say is that you should place friendship above all other human concerns. For nothing else is in such harmony with nature, nor is anything else so helpful to us in both good times and bad.

18. One thing I believe you must know above all is that friendship is not possible except between good people. Now I don't plan on going into this in depth like those who argue at length—perhaps correctly but with no thought for practical living—that only a wise man can be good. Even if we concede that they're right, they think of wisdom as a quality that no mortal man has ever truly achieved. We, on the other hand, should look instead for the kind of wisdom that can be attained in everyday life. I'd never say that even our forefathers Gaius Fabricius, Manius Curius, or Tiberius Coruncanius—all of whom our ancestors judged to be wise—reached the philosophers' standard

quidem facient; negabunt id nisi sapienti posse concedi.

19. Agamus igitur pingui, ut aiunt, Minerva: qui ita se gerunt, ita vivunt, ut eorum probetur fides integritas aequitas liberalitas, nec sit in eis ulla cupiditas libido audacia, sintque magna constantia, ut ei fuerunt modo quos nominavi, hos viros bonos, ut habiti sunt, sic etiam appellandos putemus, quia sequantur, quantum homines possunt naturam optimam bene vivendi ducem.

Sic enim mihi perspicere videor, ita natos esse nos, ut inter omnes esset societas quaedam, maior autem ut quisque proxime accederet; itaque cives potiores quam peregrini, propinqui quam alieni; cum his enim amicitiam natura

of wisdom.[23] Therefore let them keep for themselves their invidious and impossible brand of wisdom if they will only grant the Romans I just mentioned were good. They won't concede even this though, since they will say that only their kind of wise men can be good.

19. Let us therefore proceed by our own dull wits, as the saying goes. Whoever act and live so that their lives give proof of faithfulness, integrity, fairness, and generosity; and who are free from any low passion, greed, or violence; and are of great strength of character, such as those men I mentioned above—let us believe that these men should be called good, as they were considered in life, and let us call them such because as much as human beings possibly can, they followed nature, the best guide for living well.

It seems to me that we were created in such a way so that there is a bond between us all that

ipsa peperit. Sed ea non satis habet firmitatis; namque hoc praestat amicitia propinquitati, quod ex propinquitate benevolentia tolli potest, ex amicitia non potest; sublata enim benevolentia amicitiae nomen tollitur, propinquitatis manet.

20. Quanta autem vis amicitiae sit, ex hoc intellegi maxime potest, quod ex infinita societate generis humani, quam conciliavit ipsa natura, ita contracta res est et adducta in angustum, ut omnis caritas aut inter duos aut inter paucos iungeretur.

Est enim amicitia nihil aliud nisi omnium divinarum humanarumque rerum cum benevolentia et caritate consensio; qua quidem haud

grows stronger the closer we are to each other. Thus we prefer our fellow countrymen to foreigners, just as we prefer our relatives to strangers, since with these nature herself has produced a friendship of sorts. But it is not firm and constant. Friendship, however, is stronger than kinship since goodwill can be removed from such a relationship but not from friendship. If goodwill is removed from friendship, friendship disappears. However, if you remove goodwill from kinship, it nonetheless remains.

20. The power of friendship is most clearly recognized in the fact that of the infinite types of human relationships which nature herself has created, friendship is selective so that its affection joins together only two or at most a few people.

Friendship is nothing other than agreement with goodwill and affection between people about all things divine and human. With the

scio an excepta sapientia nihil melius homini sit a dis immortalibus datum. Divitias alii praeponunt, bonam alii valetudinem, alii potentiam, alii honores, multi etiam voluptates: beluarum hoc quidem extremum; illa autem superiora caduca et incerta, posita non tam in consiliis nostris quam in fortunae temeritate. Qui autem in virtute summum bonum ponunt, praeclare illi quidem, sed haec ipsa virtus amicitiam et gignit et continet nec sine virtute amicitia esse ullo pacto potest.

21. Iam virtutem ex consuetudine vitae sermonisque nostri interpretemur, nec eam, ut quidam docti, verborum magnificentia metiamur, virosque bonos eos qui habentur numeremus: Paulos, Catones, Galos, Scipiones, Philos.

exception of wisdom, I'm inclined to believe that the immortal gods have given nothing better to humanity than friendship. Some people prefer riches, others good health, some power, others honors, and many seek out sensual pleasure above all else—the last a desire fit more for beasts than human beings. All these are fleeting and uncertain goals dependent not on our reason but on the whims of fortune. But there are others who believe that the highest goal is goodness or what we call virtue. These people hold the right view, for virtue itself gives birth to friendship and nourishes it, so that without virtue friendship is not able to exist.

21. And as we said before, when we speak of virtue let us please use the term as we would in our everyday life and speech, not in the pompous and exalted ways of those learned scholars. Let us include among good men those who are

His communis vita contenta est, eos autem omittamus qui omnino nusquam reperiuntur.

22. Talis igitur inter viros amicitia tantas opportunitates habet quantas vix queo dicere. Principio qui potest esse vita vitalis, ut ait Ennius, quae non in amici mutua benevolentia conquiescit? Quid dulcius quam habere quicum omnia audeas sic loqui ut tecum? Qui esset tantus fructus in prosperis rebus nisi haberes qui illis aeque ac tu ipse gauderet? Adversas vero ferre difficile esset sine eo qui illas gravius etiam quam tu ferret. Denique ceterae res quae expetuntur opportunae sunt singulae rebus fere singulis: divitiae ut utare, opes ut colare, honores ut laudere, voluptates ut gaudeas, valetudo ut dolore careas et muneribus fungare corporis. Amicitia res plurimas continet, quoquo te

generally considered to be so—men like Paulus, Cato, Galus, Scipio, and Philus—who meet the common standard of goodness. Let's forget about the ones who are nowhere to be found in the real world.

22. Therefore among such good people as we were discussing, friendship offers benefits that I can scarcely describe. In the first place, how can life be worth living, as Ennius[24] says, unless it relies on the mutual goodwill of a friend? What could be sweeter than to have someone you can dare to talk to about everything as if you were speaking to yourself? How could you enjoy the good times of life if you didn't have someone who was as happy about your good fortune as you are? And adversity would be a terrible thing to bear unless you had someone who felt its weight even more than you.

Almost all the things we desire in life have as their aim a single end: riches are for buying

verteris praesto est, nullo loco excluditur, numquam intempestiva, numquam molesta est. Itaque non aqua, non igni, ut aiunt, locis pluribus utimur quam amicitia (neque ego nunc de vulgari aut de mediocri, quae tamen ipsa et delectat et prodest, sed de vera et perfecta loquor, qualis eorum qui pauci nominantur fuit); nam et secundas res splendidiores facit amicitia, et adversas partiens communicansque leviores.

23. Cumque plurimas et maximas commoditates amicitia contineat, tum illa nimirum praestat omnibus, quod bona spe praelucet in

things, power is for gaining influence, public office is for increasing reputation, sensual pleasures are for enjoyment, health is for freedom from pain and to fully enjoy the use of the body. Friendship, however, serves a multitude of purposes. Wherever you turn, there it is. No door shuts it out, no time is wrong for it, and never is it in the way. We need friendship in every part of our life as much as we need the proverbial water and fire, the two necessities of life. I'm not speaking now of ordinary and common friendship—as pleasant and useful as that can be—but of true and pure friendship, such as that which exists among the best of friends. This kind of friendship makes our good days shine more brightly and helps us bear the burden of our difficult times.

23. Since friendship has so many and such great advantages, it exceeds other virtues by far, especially as it shines a bright light of hope into

posterum, nec debilitari animos aut cadere patitur. Verum enim amicum qui intuetur, tamquam exemplar aliquod intuetur sui. Quocirca et absentes adsunt, et egentes abundant, et imbecilli valent et, quod difficilius dictu est, mortui vivunt: tantus eos honos, memoria, desiderium prosequitur amicorum, ex quo illorum beata mors videtur, horum vita laudabilis. Quod si exemeris ex rerum natura benevolentiae iunctionem, nec domus ulla nec urbs stare poterit, ne agri quidem cultus permanebit. Id si minus intellegitur, quanta vis amicitiae concordiaeque sit, ex dissensionibus atque ex discordiis percipi potest. Quae enim domus tam stabilis, quae tam firma civitas est, quae non odiis et discidiis funditus possit everti? Ex quo quantum boni sit in amicitia iudicari potest.

the future and does not suffer our spirits to stumble or fall. You see, whoever looks upon a true friend looks, in a sense, at an image of himself.

Even when friends are absent, they are still present. When you lack the necessities of life, with a friend you have more than enough. With such a friend, you are strong even when you are weak. And—though this is more difficult to say—when friends have died, yet they are still alive in you. So powerful and real are the memories of true friends, so great and tender is the longing for them, that even in death they are a blessing and live in us.

If you took away the bond of goodwill from the world, no house or city could stand, nor would the fields any longer bear fruit. If that statement is difficult, then consider the power of friendship by looking at the effect of its opposites, dissension and discord. What house is

24. Agrigentinum quidem doctum quendam virum carminibus Graecis vaticinatum ferunt, quae in rerum natura totoque mundo constarent quaeque moverentur, ea contrahere amicitiam, dissipare discordiam.

Atque hoc quidem omnes mortales et intellegunt et re probant. Itaque si quando aliquod officium exstitit amici in periculis aut adeundis aut communicandis, quis est qui id non maximis efferat laudibus? Qui clamores tota cavea nuper in hospitis et amici mei Marci Pacuvi nova fabula! cum ignorante rege uter Orestes esset, Pylades Orestem se esse diceret ut pro illo necaretur, Orestes autem ita ut erat, Orestem se esse perseveraret. Stantes plaudebant in re ficta: quid arbitramur in vera facturos fuisse? Facile

so secure, what city so firmly established, that hatred and division cannot destroy them? By this fact you can judge the good of their opposite—friendship.

24. They say that a certain learned man from Agrigentum sang an inspired song in Greek verse claiming that all things in nature and indeed the whole universe, whether stationary or in motion, are held together by friendship and torn apart by discord.[25] This at least is a philosopher everyone can understand and agree with. When someone does a great service or takes a great risk for a friend, who doesn't shower that person with the highest praise? What shouts rang out through the whole theater during the performance of the play written by my guest and friend Marcus Pacuvius![26] In this scene the king—who doesn't know which man is Orestes or Pylades—orders Orestes to die, but Pylades claims to be his friend in order to save him,

indicabat ipsa natura vim suam, cum homines quod facere ipsi non possent, id recte fieri in altero iudicarent.

Hactenus mihi videor de amicitia quid sentirem potuisse dicere: si qua praeterea sunt (credo autem esse multa) ab eis, si videbitur, qui ista disputant, quaeritote.

25. Fannius: Nos autem a te potius; quamquam etiam ab istis saepe quaesivi et audivi, non invitus equidem; sed aliud quoddam filum orationis tuae.

Scaevola: Tum magis id diceres, Fanni, si nuper in hortis Scipionis, cum est de re publica

while Orestes maintains that he himself should die. The people in the audience rose to their feet and cheered though it was only a play. Imagine what they would they have done if it were real life! Nature herself was exerting her power in this case by prompting those watching to approve in others a deed of true friendship they might not be able to do themselves.

Well, it seems to me I have now said to you both what I believe about friendship. If there is more to say on the subject—and I believe there is a great deal—you should seek out those skilled in such discussions.

25. *Fannius*: We would rather hear from you, Laelius. I've often sought out and listened to the kind of men you mention. I've heard them gladly, but you have a way of getting to the heart of things.

Scaevola: You would stress that point even more, Fannius, if you had been with us the other

disputatum, adfuisses: qualis tum patronus ius-
titiae fuit contra accuratam orationem Phili!

Fannius: Facile id quidem fuit, iustitiam, ius-
tissimo viro, defendere.

Scaevola: Quid amicitiam? nonne facile ei qui
ob eam summa fide constantia iustitiaque ser-
vatam maximam gloriam ceperit?

26. Laelius: Vim hoc quidem est adferre!
Quid enim refert qua me ratione cogatis? cogi-
tis certe; studiis enim generorum, praesertim in
re bona, cum difficile est, tum ne aequum quidem
obsistere.

Saepissime igitur mihi de amicitia cogitanti
maxime illud considerandum videri solet, utrum
propter imbecillitatem atque inopiam desiderata
sit amicitia, ut dandis recipiendisque meritis,
quod quis minus per se ipse posset, id acciperet

day in the country house of Scipio while they were discussing state affairs. Laelius spoke so clearly on behalf of justice compared to the elaborate arguments of Philus!

Fannius: I have no doubt it was easy for Laelius, the most just of men, to defend justice.

Scaevola: Then what about friendship? Won't it be just as easy for him, since he has the greatest reputation as a friend because of his faithfulness, perseverance, and fairness?

26. *Laelius*: You're using force to get me to speak! I'm not sure it really matters what means you use, but you are certainly coercing me. Ah well, it's for a good cause and at the bidding of my own sons-in-law, men that it is difficult and perhaps not even right to refuse.

The more I think about friendship, the more often I wonder whether the desire for friendship comes merely from our own weakness and need, so that by giving and receiving favors we

ab alio vicissimque redderet, an esset hoc quidem proprium amicitiae, sed antiquior et pulchrior et magis a natura ipsa profecta alia causa. Amor enim, ex quo amicitia nominata est, princeps est ad benevolentiam coniungendam; nam utilitates quidem etiam ab iis percipiuntur saepe qui simulatione amicitiae coluntur et observantur temporis causa; in amicitia autem nihil fictum est, nihil simulatum, et quidquid est, id est verum et voluntarium.

27. Quapropter a natura mihi videtur potius quam ab indigentia orta amicitia, applicatione magis animi cum quodam sensu amandi quam cogitatione quantum illa res utilitatis esset habitura.

simply grant someone the services we can provide in exchange for the things we ourselves need. This is undeniably a part of being a friend, but I wonder if there isn't a deeper and more beautiful reason for friendship than this, something that comes to us from nature herself. For it is love [*amor*] from which the word "friendship" [*amicitia*] comes, and this is the origin of goodwill. It's certainly true that people will court and flatter one another in the name of friendship to gain some advantage to suit the occasion, but in sincere friendship there is nothing false, nothing pretended. Everything in real friendship is true and genuine.

27. It seems to me that friendship arises from nature itself rather than from any need, along with an inclination of the soul joined with a sense of love rather than a calculation of how useful the relationship might be.

Quod quidem quale sit etiam in bestiis quibusdam animadverti potest, quae ex se natos ita amant ad quoddam tempus et ab eis ita amantur, ut facile earum sensus appareat; quod in homine multo est evidentius, primum ex ea caritate quae est inter natos et parentes, quae dirimi nisi detestabili scelere non potest, deinde cum similis sensus exstitit amoris, si aliquem nacti sumus cuius cum moribus et natura congruamus, quod in eo quasi lumen aliquod probitatis et virtutis perspicere videamur.

28. Nihil est enim virtute amabilius, nihil quod magis alliciat ad diligendum, quippe cum propter virtutem et probitatem etiam eos quos numquam vidimus quodam modo diligamus. Quis est qui C. Fabrici, M'. Curi non cum caritate aliqua benevola memoriam usurpet, quos numquam viderit? Quis autem est qui Tarquinium Superbum, qui Sp. Cassium, Sp. Maelium non oderit? Cum duobus ducibus de imperio in

We can see the beginnings of friendship even in certain animals, which for a certain time love their offspring and are so loved by them that the feelings are clear. It is even more evident in humans, first from the love between children and parents—which nothing but the most outrageous evil can destroy—and then from the sense of affection that arises when we meet somebody whose ways and character are aligned with our own. In such a person we see as it were the light of goodness and virtue shining forth.

28. Nothing is more appealing in another person than virtue, for nothing draws us more to love and admire someone. Even if we've never met certain people famed for goodness and virtue, we can't help but feel affection for them. Don't our hearts grow warm when we remember the stories of Gaius Fabricius or Manius Curius, although we never met them? Don't we also despise Tarquin the Proud,

Italia est decertatum, Pyrrho et Hannibale: ab altero propter probitatem eius non nimis alienos animos habemus, alterum propter crudelitatem semper haec civitas oderit.

29. Quod si tanta vis probitatis est ut eam vel in eis quos numquam vidimus, vel quod maius est in hoste etiam diligamus, quid mirum est si animi hominum moveantur, cum eorum quibuscum usu coniuncti esse possunt, virtutem et bonitatem perspicere videantur? Quamquam confirmatur amor et beneficio accepto et studio perspecto et consuetudine adiuncta; quibus rebus ad illum primum motum animi et amoris adhibitis, admirabilis quaedam exardescit benevolentiae magnitudo. Quam si qui putant ab imbecillitate proficisci, ut sit per quem adsequatur quod quisque desideret, humilem sane relinquunt et minime generosum, ut ita dicam,

Spurius Cassius, and Spurius Maelius? And remember Pyrrhus and Hannibal, the two great generals who threatened to destroy Italy. We don't really hate Pyrrhus since he was an upright man, but our country will always detest Hannibal because of his cruelty.[27]

29. Now if goodness is such a powerful force that we admire it in people we've never met and, even more remarkably, in those who are our enemies, is it any wonder that our hearts are stirred when we see virtue and excellence in someone with whom we might form a close connection? Yet love is strengthened even more by receiving kindness, by seeing the other person care for us, and by spending time together. In this way, drawn together by mutual affection, a wonderful abundance of goodwill between two people grows into a flame.

If anyone thinks that such feelings arise from weakness and are simply about gaining

ortum amicitiae, quam ex inopia atque indigentia natam volunt. Quod si ita esset, ut quisque minimum esse in se arbitraretur, ita ad amicitiam esset aptissimus; quod longe secus est.

30. Ut enim quisque sibi plurimum confidit, et ut quisque maxime virtute et sapientia sic munitus est ut nullo egeat, suaque omnia in se ipso posita iudicet, ita in amicitiis expetendis colendisque maxime excellit. Quid enim? Africanus indigens mei? Minime hercule, ac ne ego quidem illius; sed ego admiratione quadam virtutis eius, ille vicissim opinione fortasse nonnulla, quam de meis moribus habebat, me dilexit; auxit benevolentiam consuetudo; sed quamquam utilitates multae et magnae consecutae sunt, non sunt tamen ab earum spe causae diligendi profectae.

something you lack from someone else, they are granting friendship a far too humble and lowly origin. Real friendship cannot be the child of poverty and need. If this were true, the less people had, the better their qualifications for friendship would be. But this is far from the truth.

30. To the degree a person relies on himself and is made sturdy by virtue and wisdom so that he depends on no one and thus possesses all he needs within himself, to that extent he most excels at seeking out and cherishing friendships. Did my departed friend Africanus need me? By Hercules, not at all! And I had no need of him. But I loved him because of his goodness, just as he, if I judged rightly, loved me because of the virtue he saw in me. And as we got to know one another better, our affection for each other grew. Of course, there were many practical advantages to our friendship, but our

31. Ut enim benefici liberalesque sumus non ut exigamus gratiam (neque enim beneficium feneramur, sed natura propensi ad liberalitatem sumus), sic amicitiam non spe mercedis adducti, sed quod omnis eius fructus in ipso amore inest, expetendam putamus.

32. Ab his, qui pecudum ritu ad voluptatem omnia referunt, longe dissentiunt; nec mirum; nihil enim altum, nihil magnificum ac divinum suspicere possunt, qui suas omnes cogitationes abiecerunt in rem tam humilem tamque contemptam. Quam ob rem hos quidem ab hoc sermone removeamus, ipsi autem intellegamus natura gigni sensum diligendi et benevolentiae caritatem, facta significatione probitatis.

Quam qui adpetiverunt, applicant se et propius admovent, ut et usu eius quem diligere

mutual love was not based on what we might gain from each other.

31. We are not kind and generous to our friends because we seek favors in return. We are not so petty as to charge interest on our kindness. We are kindhearted because it is the right and natural thing to do, not because we are hoping for something in return. The reward of friendship is friendship itself.

32. Those who like cattle judge everything in terms of how much pleasure it gives them will surely disagree. This is no surprise. It is impossible for these people who have lowered their minds to such a degraded level to raise their heads up to gaze at anything lofty, noble, and divine. Let us not trouble ourselves about such people in this conversation. Instead let us trust that our feelings of love and affection for those we judge to be good people spring from nature itself.

coeperunt fruantur et moribus, sintque pares in amore et aequales, propensioresque ad bene merendum quam ad reposcendum, atque haec inter eos sit honesta certatio. Sic et utilitates ex amicitia maximae capientur, et erit eius ortus a natura quam ab imbecillitate gravior et verior. Nam si utilitas amicitias conglutinaret, eadem commutata dissolveret; sed quia natura mutari non potest, idcirco verae amicitiae sempiternae sunt. Ortum quidem amicitiae videtis, nisi quid ad haec forte vultis.

Fannius: Tu vero perge, Laeli; pro hoc enim, qui minor est natu, meo iure respondeo.

When two people long for such goodness, they seek it out in each other and so draw closer together, so that they can enjoy the company and character of the one they love. They become rivals in doing good for each other, more desirous of doing good for the other than getting something in return—an honorable competition! In this way friendship becomes something quite advantageous, not in the sense of gaining something we need in our weakness but as a relationship deriving from nature itself. If we assume friendship is based merely on gaining advantages from someone, then that friendship will end when that person has nothing left to give us. But since nature cannot be changed, real friendships last forever.

That is what I think about the origins of friendship. Do you wish to say anything before I continue?

33. Scaevola: Recte tu quidem; quam ob rem audiamus.

Laelius: Audite vero, optimi viri, ea quae saepissime inter me et Scipionem de amicitia disserebantur. Quamquam ille quidem nihil difficilius esse dicebat quam amicitiam usque ad extremum vitae diem permanere; nam vel ut non idem expediret, incidere saepe, vel ut de re publica non idem sentiretur; mutari etiam mores hominum saepe dicebat, alias adversis rebus, alias aetate ingravescente. Atque earum rerum exemplum ex similitudine capiebat ineuntis aetatis, quod summi puerorum amores saepe una cum praetexta toga ponerentur.

34. Sin autem ad adulescentiam perduxissent, dirimi tamen interdum contentione, vel uxoriae condicionis vel commodi alicuius quod idem

Fannius: Please do continue, Laelius. I believe I speak for my younger friend here as well.

33. *Scaevola*: Indeed you do. We would both like to hear more.

Laelius: Then listen, gentlemen, to what Scipio and I discussed during our frequent conversations on friendship. He used to say that nothing was more difficult than for two people to remain friends until the end of their lives. Either the friendship would end when their lives changed somehow, or they would have a falling out over politics, as often happens, or they would simply drift apart because of some adversity or the increasing burdens of old age. He used to compare it to the changes that take place when we put away the things we loved most as boys and put on the toga of manhood.

34. If a friendship can survive until young adulthood, then it might still be torn apart by rivalry for the same woman or for some

adipisci uterque non posset. Quod si qui longius in amicitia provecti essent, tamen saepe labefactari si in honoris contentionem incidissent; pestem enim nullam maiorem esse amicitiis quam in plerisque pecuniae cupiditatem, in optimis quibusque honoris certamen et gloriae, ex quo inimicitias maximas saepe inter amicissimos exstitisse.

35. Magna etiam discidia et plerumque iusta nasci, cum aliquid ab amicis quod rectum non esset postularetur, ut aut libidinis ministri aut adiutores essent ad iniuriam; quod qui recusarent, quamvis honeste id facerent, ius tamen amicitiae deserere arguerentur ab eis quibus obsequi nollent. Illos autem, qui quidvis ab amico auderent postulare, postulatione ipsa profiteri omnia se amici causa esse facturos; eorum querella non inveteratas modo familiaritates exstingui solere, sed odia etiam gigni sempiterna.

advantage that both men can't have. If friendship can last into the prime of life, then it can collapse because of competition for the same political office. Certainly most friendships among common people end because of the desire for money, but among the better class of men friendships die because of the fight over honor and glory, which often causes the best of friends to become the worst of enemies.

35. A serious and justifiable division can arise between friends when one asks the other to do something that is not right, such as to help arrange some shameful sexual rendezvous or to engage in an act of violence. The friends who excuse themselves from such activities, even if they are acting honorably, are likely to be charged with violating the law of friendship by those they turn down. After all, those who would make such demands show that they themselves would be willing to do anything for

Haec ita multa quasi fata impendere amicitiis ut omnia subterfugere non modo sapientiae sed etiam felicitatis diceret sibi videri.

36. Quam ob rem id primum videamus, si placet, quatenus amor in amicitia progredi debeat. Numne si Coriolanus habuit amicos, ferre contra patriam arma illi cum Coriolano debuerunt? Num Vecellinum amici, regnum appetentem, num Maelium debuerunt iuvare?

37. Tiberium quidem Gracchum rem publicam vexantem a Q. Tuberone aequalibusque amicis derelictum videbamus; at C. Blossius Cumanus, hospes familiae vestrae, Scaevola, cum ad me (quod aderam Laenati et Rupilio consulibus in consilio) deprecatum venisset,

their friends. But by these repeated requests not only are friendships destroyed, but lifelong hatred between former friends can arise. Scipio would often say that such dangers hover like the dreaded goddesses of fate over friendship, so that it requires both wisdom and luck to escape them all.

36. So if you both don't mind, let's first consider how far devotion ought to go in friendship. If Coriolanus had any friends, shouldn't they have taken up arms against their own country alongside him?[28] Shouldn't the friends of Vecellinus or Maelius have helped them try to overthrow the Republic and become kings of Rome?

37. In our own time we saw Tiberius Gracchus start a revolution against the state, during which he was abandoned by Quintus Tubero and other friends his own age. And yet Gaius Blossius of Cumae—a guest of your own family, Scaevola—came to me after the arrest of

hanc ut sibi ignoscerem causam adferebat, quod tanti Tiberium Gracchum fecisset ut quidquid ille vellet sibi faciendum putaret. Tum ego: 'Etiamne si te in Capitolium faces ferre vellet?' 'Numquam' inquit 'voluisset id quidem; sed si voluisset, paruissem.'

Videtis quam nefaria vox! Et hercule ita fecit, vel plus etiam quam dixit; non enim paruit ille Tiberii Gracchi temeritati, sed praefuit, nec se comitem illius furoris sed ducem praebuit. Itaque hac amentia, quaestione nova perterritus, in Asiam profugit, ad hostes se contulit, poenas rei publicae graves iustasque persolvit.

Nulla est igitur excusatio peccati si amici causa peccaveris; nam cum conciliatrix amicitiae virtutis opinio fuerit, difficile est amicitiam manere si a virtute defeceris.

Gracchus while I was meeting with the consuls Laenas and Rupilius to plead for leniency for himself on the grounds that he held Gracchus in such high esteem that it was his duty to do anything he asked of him.[29] I asked him, "What if Gracchus had asked you to set fire to the Capitol?" He answered, "Gracchus never would have asked *that* of me—but if he had, I would have burned it down."

Do you see what a wicked answer that was? By Hercules, he did everything he said he would and more! He didn't just follow Gracchus in his rashness, but he surpassed him and became a leader in that madness. He became deranged in his passion and fled into Asia when threatened by a special court of inquiry. There he joined our enemies and paid a heavy and just price for his crimes against our Republic.

Doing wrong for the sake of a friend never justifies that wrong. Remember that friendship

38. Quod si rectum statuerimus vel concedere amicis quidquid velint, vel impetrare ab eis quidquid velimus, perfecta quidem sapientia si simus, nihil habeat res vitii. Sed loquimur de eis amicis qui ante oculos sunt, quos vidimus aut de quibus memoria accepimus, quos novit vita communis; ex hoc numero nobis exempla sumenda sunt, et eorum quidem maxime qui ad sapientiam proxime accedunt.

39. Videmus Papum Aemilium Luscino familiarem fuisse (sic a patribus accepimus), bis una consules, collegas in censura; tum et cum eis et inter se coniunctissimos fuisse Manium Curium, Tiberium Coruncanium memoriae proditum est. Igitur ne suspicari quidem possumus quemquam horum ab amico quidpiam

is founded on virtue. If a friend expects you to do something evil, it is difficult for that friendship to continue.

38. If we decided it was right to do for friends whatever they wished and to get from them whatever we wish, no harm would come of it— but only if we were perfect in our wisdom. However, we're talking now about the kind of friends we see before our eyes or those we know about, the kind of friends that exist in real life, not in some ideal world. It's from these real people we should draw our examples, especially those who come closest to true wisdom.

39. We've read in the writings of our ancestors that Aemilius Papus was a close friend of Gaius Luscinus. Twice they were consuls together and also served together as censors. We have read as well that Manius Curius and Tiberius Coruncanius were friends with them and with each other. It is impossible to believe that

contendisse quod contra fidem, contra ius iurandum, contra rem publicam esset. Nam hoc quidem in talibus viris quid attinet dicere, si contendisset impetraturum non fuisse, cum illi sanctissimi viri fuerint, aeque autem nefas sit tale aliquid et facere rogatum et rogare? At vero Tiberium Gracchum sequebantur C. Carbo, C. Cato et minime tum quidem Gaius frater, nunc idem acerrimus.

40. Haec igitur lex in amicitia sanciatur, ut neque rogemus res turpes, nec faciamus rogati. Turpis enim excusatio est et minime accipienda, cum in ceteris peccatis, tum si quis contra rem publicam se amici causa fecisse fateatur.

Etenim eo loco, Fanni et Scaevola, locati sumus, ut nos longe prospicere oporteat futuros casus rei publicae. Deflexit iam aliquantum de spatio curriculoque consuetudo maiorum.

any of these men would ever do anything for a friend that was unjust, involved breaking an oath, or would harm the Republic. In the case of men like these, why even bother to point out that, if someone had made such a request, it would not have been granted? Men so noble would consider it just as wrong to ask for such a favor as to grant one. Yet Gaius Carbo and Gaius Cato did follow Tiberius Gracchus, as did his brother Gaius, reluctantly at first but then with enthusiasm.[30]

40. Therefore let this be a law of friendship: Never ask a friend to do anything shameful, and don't do anything shameful if asked. Moreover, as disgraceful as it is in general to do something shameful because of friendship, it is inexcusable when someone says he harmed the Republic for the sake of a friend.

My friends, we live in a time when we ought to be especially aware of threats to our country,

41. Tiberius Gracchus regnum occupare conatus est, vel regnavit is quidem paucos menses: numquid simile populus Romanus audierat aut viderat? Hunc etiam post mortem secuti amici et propinqui quid in Publio Nasica effecerint, sine lacrimis non queo dicere. Nam Carbonem, quoquo modo potuimus, propter recentem poenam Ti. Gracchi sustinuimus; de Gai Gracchi autem tribunatu quid expectem, non libet augurari. Serpit deim e dei res quae proclivis ad perniciem, cum semel coepit, labitur. Videtis in tabella iam ante quanta sit facta labes, primo Gabinia lege, biennio post Cassia. Videre iam videor populum a senatu disiunctum, multitudinis arbitrio res maximas agi; plures enim discent quem ad modum haec fiant, quam quem ad modum his resistatur.

for we have wandered far from the path laid out by those who came before us.

41. Tiberius Gracchus tried to rule as king—or I should say he actually did rule for a few months. The Roman people had never heard or seen anything like it before. What his friends and relatives who continued to follow his cause after his death did to Publius Scipio I can't describe without tears. As for Carbo, we've put up with him as best we could since the punishment of Tiberius Gracchus was so recent. What we can expect from Gaius Gracchus when he becomes tribune, I don't care to foretell. Events creep along from day to day now, but once they have built up momentum they slide headlong into ruin. You see what a disaster the issue of the ballot has become, first with the Gabinian Law then two years later with the Cassian.[31] It seems to me the people have been set at odds with the Senate and the most important affairs

42. Quorsum haec? Quia sine sociis nemo quidquam tale conatur. Praecipiendum est igitur bonis, ut si in eiusmodi amicitias ignari casu aliquo inciderint, ne existiment ita se alligatos ut ab amicis in magna aliqua re peccantibus non discedant; improbis autem poena statuenda est, nec vero minor eis qui secuti erunt alterum quam eis qui ipsi fuerint impietatis duces. Quis clarior in Graecia Themistocle, quis potentior? qui cum imperator bello Persico servitute Graeciam liberavisset, propterque invidiam in exsilium expulsus esset, ingratae patriae iniuriam non tulit quam ferre debuit: fecit idem quod viginti annis ante apud nos fecerat Coriolanus. His adiutor contra patriam inventus est nemo; itaque mortem sibi uterque conscivit.

of state are decided by the whim of the mob. More people will learn how to start this kind of trouble than will learn how to resist it.

42. Why do I say these things? Because without accomplices no one tries to do such terrible deeds. Therefore when good people realize they have fallen in with such people by chance, they must know that they are not bound by friendship to commit some act of treachery against their country. Traitors must be punished, but no less a punishment should befall those who follow them in wickedness. Who was more famous or powerful in Greece than Themistocles? He rescued Greece from slavery during the war with Persia, but then on account of his unpopularity he went into exile, not willing to bearing the injustice of his ungrateful country as was his duty. He acted in the same way Coriolanus did in our own land twenty years earlier. No

43. Quare talis improborum consensio non modo excusatione amicitiae tegenda non est, sed potius supplicio omni vindicanda est, ut ne quis concessum putet amicum vel bellum patriae inferentem sequi; quod quidem, ut res ire coepit, haud scio an aliquando futurum sit; mihi autem non minori curae est qualis res publica post mortem meam futura, quam qualis hodie sit.

44. Haec igitur prima lex amicitiae sanciatur, ut ab amicis honesta petamus, amicorum causa honesta faciamus; ne exspectemus quidem dum rogemur; studium semper adsit, cunctatio absit; consilium vero dare audeamus libere; plurimum in amicitia amicorum bene suadentium valeat auctoritas; eaque et adhibeatur ad monendum,

one was willing to help these men fight against their countries, so both men in the end killed themselves.[32]

43. Therefore a plea of friendship should never be offered as an excuse for such wicked conspiracies. I believe they should be punished to the full extent of the law so that no one ever thinks it is forgivable to aid a friend in a plot against one's own country—a thing which, as matters are going, I'd not be surprised to see happen in the future. After all, I'm worried about the fate of the Republic after my death as much as I am about the present.

44. Therefore, as I have said, let this be ordained as the first law of friendship: Seek from friends only what is honorable and do for friends only what is just—but don't wait to be asked. Let your eagerness always be present and hesitation absent. Give your honest advice freely. Among friends, always listen to the counsel of

non modo aperte sed etiam acriter, si res postulabit, et adhibitae pareatur.

45. Nam quibusdam, quos audio sapientes habitos in Graecia, placuisse opinor mirabilia quaedam (sed nihil est quod illi non persequantur argutiis): partim fugiendas esse nimias amicitias, ne necesse sit unum sollicitum esse pro pluribus; satis superque esse sibi suarum cuique rerum, alienis nimis implicari molestum esse; commodissimum esse quam laxissimas habenas habere amicitiae, quas vel adducas cum velis, vel remittas; caput enim esse ad beate vivendum securitatem, qua frui non possit animus si tamquam parturiat unus pro pluribus.

your wise companions. True friends should give faithful advice to each other, not only with frankness but with sternness if necessary. And this advice should be heeded.

45. Now I hear there are those in Greece who are thought to be wise who say some things I find astonishing (there is no argument too subtle for them!). Some of these men say that we should avoid having too many friends, so that one person isn't burdened with anxiety. They say that each of us has more than enough concerns of his own without being burdened by the problems of others. They also say we should hold the reins of friendship loosely, so that we can draw them tight or let them go slack as we see fit. In their minds the most important thing in a good life is freedom from care, which the soul cannot enjoy when one man is in labor, so to speak, with many people's troubles.

46. Alios autem dicere aiunt, multo etiam inhumanius (quem locum breviter paulo ante perstrinxi), praesidi adiumentique causa, non benevolentiae neque caritatis, amicitias esse expetendas; itaque, ut quisque minimum firmitatis haberet minimumque virium, ita amicitias appetere maxime; ex eo fieri ut mulierculae magis amicitiarum praesidia quaerant quam viri, et inopes quam opulenti, et calamitosi quam ei qui putentur beati.

47. O praeclaram sapientiam! Solem enim e mundo tollere videntur qui amicitiam e vita tollunt, qua nihil a dis immortalibus melius habemus, nihil iucundius. Quae est enim ista securitas? Specie quidem blanda; sed reapse multis locis repudianda. Neque enim est consentaneum ullam honestam rem actionemve, ne sollicitus sis, aut non suscipere aut susceptam

46. I have heard that other people, with even more inhumanity in them, make an even worse argument, which I briefly mentioned earlier. They say that friendships should be formed for the sake of defense and the help they can give, not out of goodwill and genuine affection. In this way of thinking those with the least stability and strength are the most eager to form friendships—so that women seek out friendship more than men, or the poor more than the rich, or the miserable more than those who are considered happy.

47. O brilliant wisdom! They might as well steal the sun from the heavens as remove friendship from life! For nothing we have from the gods is better or more enjoyable than friendship. What is this "freedom from care" they seek anyway? It might seem attractive at first, but in fact it is often a thing to be shunned. It doesn't make sense to avoid some honorable

deponere; quod si curam fugimus, virtus fugienda est, quae necesse est cum aliqua cura res sibi contrarias aspernetur atque oderit, ut bonitas malitiam, temperantia libidinem, ignaviam fortitudo; itaque videas rebus iniustis iustos maxime dolere, imbellibus fortes, flagitiosis modestos; ergo hoc proprium est animi bene constituti, et laetari bonis rebus et dolere contrariis.

48. Quam ob rem si cadit in sapientem animi dolor (qui profecto cadit, nisi ex eius animo exstirpatam humanitatem arbitramur), quae causa est cur amicitiam funditus tollamus e vita, ne aliquas propter eam suscipiamus molestias? Quid enim interest, motu animi sublato, non dico inter pecudem et hominem, sed inter hominem et truncum aut saxum aut quidvis generis eiusdem? Neque enim sunt isti audiendi,

deed or action or to abandon it once we've begun just so we can be free from anxiety. If we avoid care, we avoid virtue as well, since virtue requires some care in order to reject its opposite. Goodness is eager to avoid evil, self-control to escape lust, and bravery to flee from cowardice! That's why you see the just most pained by injustice, the brave by cowardice, and the moderate by excess. It's simply a characteristic of a well-ordered mind to rejoice in what is good and grieve at the opposite.

48. So if any wise person is going to sometimes suffer distress—which each of us will unless we have driven all human feeling from our hearts—why on earth should we try to remove friendship from our lives to avoid suffering? If you take emotion away, what difference is there, not I say between a human being and a beast, but between a living person and a tree trunk or a rock or some such thing? Those men who

qui virtutem duram et quasi ferream esse quandam volunt; quae quidem est cum multis in rebus, tum in amicitia, tenera atque tractabilis, ut et bonis amici quasi diffundatur, et incommodis contrahatur. Quam ob rem angor iste qui pro amico saepe capiendus est, non tantum valet ut tollat e vita amicitiam, non plus quam ut virtutes quia nonnullas curas et molestias adferunt repudientur.

Cum autem contrahat amicitiam, ut supra dixi, si qua significatio virtutis eluceat, ad quam se similis animus applicet et adiungat, id cum contigit, amor exoriatur necesse est.

49. Quid enim tam absurdum quam delectari multis inanimis rebus, ut honore, ut gloria, ut aedificio, ut vestitu cultuque corporis, animo autem virtute praedito, eo qui vel amare vel (ut

claim that virtue is something hard and rigid like iron are not worth listening to. Truly, in many aspects of life, but especially in friendship, virtue can bend and yield so that it shapes itself to the needs of a friend in both good times and bad. Anxiety for the sake of a friend is something we should accept and certainly isn't grounds for removing friendship from our life, any more than we should reject living a virtuous life because it sometimes causes us care and distress.

But since, as I said before, virtue holds friendship together, if there should be some shining act of goodness done by one friend which the other embraces and returns, then a true love between friends will by necessity arise.

49. Is there anything more absurd than to take delight in a multitude of empty things—such as honor, glory, buildings, clothing, or bodily improvement—and yet not delight in a

ita dicam) redamare possit, non admodum de-
lectari? Nihil est enim remuneratione benevo-
lentiae, nihil vicissitudine studiorum officio-
rumque iucundius.

50. Quid si illud etiam addimus, quod recte
addi potest, nihil esse quod ad se rem ullam tam
illiciat et tam trahat quam ad amicitiam simili-
tudo? Concedetur profecto verum esse, ut bonos
boni diligant adsciscantque sibi quasi propinq-
uitate coniunctos atque natura; nihil est enim
appetentius similium sui nec rapacius quam
natura. Quam ob rem hoc quidem, Fanni et
Scaevola, constet, ut opinor: bonis inter bonos
quasi necessariam benevolentiam, qui est amici-
tiae fons a natura constitutus. Sed eadem boni-
tas etiam ad multitudines pertinet; non enim est
inhumana virtus neque immunis neque superba,
quae etiam populos universos tueri eisque op-
time consulere soleat, quod non faceret pro-
fecto si a caritate vulgi abhorreret.

living soul endowed with virtue who is capable of being loved and, if I may say so, loving in return? For nothing brings friends more joy than returning kindness and helping each other.

50. And if I may add another point, which I can rightly do, isn't it true that nothing so attracts and draws anything to itself as a likeness of feeling does in friendship? It must be granted that good people feel affection for and seek out other good people as if nature herself created the kinship between them. For there is nothing more eager and greedy than nature for things similar to itself. On account of this, my young friends, I think it's clear that good people have, so to speak, a necessary affection for good people, because nature has established this as the source of friendship. But we should be clear that the quality of goodness belongs to all kinds of people. Virtue isn't something inhuman, exclusive, or proud, but a force that protects

51. Atque etiam mihi quidem videntur qui utilitatum causa fingunt amicitias, amabilissimum nodum amicitiae tollere. Non enim tam utilitas parta per amicum, quam amici amor ipse delectat; tumque illud fit quod ab amico est profectum iucundum, si cum studio est profectum; tantumque abest ut amicitiae propter indigentiam colantur, ut ei qui opibus et copiis, maximeque virtute (in qua plurimum est praesidi), minime alterius indigeant, liberalissimi sint et beneficentissimi. Atque haud sciam an ne opus sit quidem nihil umquam omnino deesse amicis; ubi enim studia nostra viguissent, si numquam consilio, numquam opera nostra nec domi nec militiae Scipio eguisset? Non igitur utilitatem amicitia, sed utilitas amicitiam secuta est.

entire nations and looks after their well-being—
something it certainly wouldn't do if it shunned
the affection of the common people.

51. And again it seems to me that those who
say advantage is the basis of friendship would
destroy its most precious bond. It isn't so much
the advantage gained from a friend that delights
us as the friend's love itself. The practical ad-
vantage we receive from a friend is a pleasure
only when it is freely and joyfully given. It
simply isn't true that real friendship is culti-
vated because of need. The kindest and most
generous people are actually those who need
the other person the least, that is, those who are
richest in wealth and power—and especially in
virtue, the best defense a person can have. Yet I
don't think it follows that friends should never
need anything at all from one another. How
could I have ever shown my commitment to
him if Scipio had never needed my advice or

52. Non ergo erunt homines deliciis difflu-
entes audiendi, si quando de amicitia, quam nec
usu nec ratione habent cognitam, disputabunt.
Nam quis est, pro deorum fidem atque homi-
num! qui velit, ut neque diligat quemquam nec
ipse ab ullo diligatur, circumfluere omnibus
copiis atque in omnium rerum abundantia viv-
ere? Haec enim est tyrannorum vita nimirum,
in qua nulla fides, nulla caritas, nulla stabilis be-
nevolentiae potest esse fiducia: omnia semper
suspecta atque sollicita, nullus locus amicitiae.

53. quis enim aut eum diligat quem metuat,
aut eum a quo se metui putet? Coluntur tamen
simulatione dumtaxat ad tempus; quod si
forte, ut fit plerumque, ceciderunt, tum intel-
legitur quam fuerint inopes amicorum; quod

assistance at home or abroad? Put concisely, friendship doesn't result from advantage, but advantage results from friendship.

52. So we won't pay any attention to those who seek only after pleasure when they talk about friendship, since they understand it neither in theory nor in practice. By gods and men! Who is there who would wish to be surrounded by all the riches in the world and enjoy every abundance in life and yet not love or be loved by anyone? Surely this is the life of a tyrant, a life in which there is no trust, no mutual affection, no expectation of kindness. Where all is anxiety and suspicion, there is no place for friendship.

53. How can anyone love a person he fears, or love someone who fears him? Tyrants seem to be loved, but only for a time. When they fall from power, as they almost always do, then they discover how few friends they have. It's

Tarquinium dixisse ferunt exsulantem, tum se intellexisse quos fidos amicos habuisset, quos infidos, cum iam neutris gratiam referre posset;

54. quamquam miror, illa superbia et importunitate, si quemquam amicum habere potuit; atque ut huius quem dixi mores veros amicos parare non potuerunt, sic multorum opes praepotentium excludunt amicitias fideles. Non enim solum ipsa Fortuna caeca est, sed eos etiam plerumque efficit caecos quos complexa est; itaque efferuntur fere fastidio et contumacia, nec quidquam insipiente fortunato intolerabilius fieri potest. Atque hoc quidem videre licet, eos qui antea commodis fuerint moribus, imperio potestate, prosperis rebus immutari, sperni ab iis veteres amicitias, indulgeri novis.

said that when Tarquin [the last king of Rome] went into exile, he confessed that it was only then he knew which of his friends were faithful and which were not, since he was no longer able to reward anyone.

54. Actually I'm amazed that Tarquin had any friends at all given his arrogance and cruelty. And just as his character made it impossible for him to have any true friends, so too the wealth and power of men often prevent them from developing any loyal friendships. Not only is Fortune blind herself, but she frequently blinds those she loves. They get carried away by their own obstinacy and pride—and nothing is more unbearable than a fortunate fool. Indeed, we often see people once gracious and kind but now having gained position, power, and wealth abandon their old friends and delight in new ones.

55. Quid autem stultius quam cum pluri-
mum copiis facultatibus opibus possint, cetera
parare quae parantur pecunia—equos, famulos,
vestem egregiam, vasa pretiosa—amicos non
parare, optimam et pulcherrimam vitae, ut ita
dicam, supellectilem? Etenim cetera cum parant,
cui parent nesciunt, nec cuius causa laborent;
eius enim est istorum quidque qui vicit viribus;
amicitiarum sua cuique permanet stabilis et
certa possessio, ut etiamsi illa maneant quae
sunt quasi dona fortunae, tamen vita inculta et
deserta ab amicis non possit esse iucunda.

Sed haec hactenus.

56. Constituendi autem sunt qui sint in
amicitia fines et quasi termini diligendi. De
quibus tres video sententias ferri, quarum nul-
lam probo: unam ut eodem modo erga amicum

55. What could be more foolish than for a person with an abundance of wealth, skills, and resources to acquire all the things money can buy—horses, slaves, fine clothing, expensive dining ware—and yet not acquire friends? After all, friends are the finest and most beautiful adornment of life. When such people are buying all those other things, they don't really know who will get them or for whose benefit they are working so hard, for such things often end up in the hands of the strongest. But friends are the most sure and stable possession anyone can have. Even if someone has all the riches fortune can give, a life without the joys of friendship is empty and miserable.

But enough on this point.

56. Consider with me now the limits and, so to speak, boundary stones of friendship. I'm aware of three opinions on the subject, none of which I agree with. First, that we should care

adfecti simus quo erga nosmet ipsos; alteram ut
nostra in amicos benevolentia illorum erga nos
benevolentiae pariter aequaliterque respondeat;
tertiam ut quanti quisque se ipse facit, tanti fiat
ab amicis.

57. Harum trium sententiarum nulli prorsus
assentior. Nec enim illa prima vera est, ut quem
ad modum in se quisque sit, sic in amicum sit
animatus: quam multa enim, quae nostra causa
numquam faceremus, facimus causa amicorum:
precari ab indigno, supplicare, tum acerbius in
aliquem invehi insectarique vehementius; quae
in nostris rebus non satis honeste, in amicorum
fiunt honestissime. Multaeque res sunt in qui-
bus de suis commodis viri boni multa detrahunt
detrahique patiuntur, ut eis amici potius quam
ipsi fruantur.

about our friends in the same way we care about ourselves. Second, that our goodwill toward our friends should be exactly equal to their goodwill toward us. Third, that whatever value a man puts on himself, his friends should do the same.

57. I think all three of these views are wrong. The first—that we should do for our friends as we would do for ourselves—is certainly false. Think how much we do for our friends that we would never do for ourselves! For a friend we will beg and plead with some unworthy person, or we will challenge or confront someone quite harshly and loudly. It wouldn't be honorable to do this for ourselves, but it is most honorable when we do it for a friend. Good men will often put themselves at a disadvantage and give up things they want and need, so that their friends, rather than themselves, can enjoy them.

58. Altera sententia est quae definit amicitiam paribus officiis ac voluntatibus. Hoc quidem est nimis exigue et exiliter ad calculos vocare amicitiam, ut par sit ratio acceptorum et datorum. Divitior mihi et affluentior videtur esse vera amicitia, nec observare restricte ne plus reddat quam acceperit; neque enim verendum est ne quid excidat, aut ne quid in terram defluat, aut ne plus aequo quid in amicitiam congeratur.

59. Tertius vero ille finis deterrimus, ut quanti quisque se ipse faciat, tanti fiat ab amicis. Saepe enim in quibusdam aut animus abiectior est, aut spes amplificandae fortunae fractior. Non est igitur amici talem esse in eum qualis ille in se est, sed potius eniti et efficere ut amici iacentem animum excitet, inducatque in spem cogitationemque meliorem.

58. The second view limits friendship to an equal exchange of actions and feelings. This reduces friendship to a careful and petty calculation of credits and debits. I think that true friendship is something richer and more abundant than that. It doesn't check the books to see if it's giving more than it has received; it doesn't fear that some favor will get lost or overflow and spill onto the ground, or that it's pouring more into the other's bowl than it's getting back.

59. But the third view—that someone should be valued by his friends just as much as he values himself—is the worst of all. For often the spirit of friends is broken, and they have little faith that their fortunes will improve. In these cases it's not the mark of a friend to have the same judgment of another as he does of himself, but rather to work mightily to raise his spirits and lead him to better hopes and plans.

Alius igitur finis verae amicitiae constituendus est, si prius quid maxime reprehendere Scipio solitus sit edixero. Negabat ullam vocem inimiciorem amicitiae potuisse reperiri, quam eius qui dixisset ita amare oportere, ut si aliquando esset osurus; nec vero se adduci posse ut hoc, quem ad modum putaretur, a Biante esse dictum crederet, qui sapiens habitus esset unus e Septem: impuri cuiusdam aut ambitiosi aut omnia ad suam potentiam revocantis esse sententiam. Quonam enim modo quisquam amicus esse poterit eius cui se putabit inimicum esse posse? Quin etiam necesse erit cupere et optare ut quam saepissime peccet amicus, quo plures det sibi tamquam ansas ad reprehendendum; rursum autem recte factis commodisque amicorum necesse erit angi, dolere, invidere.

So we must find a better way to describe the limits of friendships—but first I want to deal with a belief that Scipio condemned vehemently. He often said that no precept was more contrary to friendship than the one saying we should love a friend as if someday we might hate him. Scipio could never be convinced that this proverb came, as many believe, from Bias, who was counted as one of the Seven Sages. He believed that it was put forward by some wretched, scheming, or utterly selfish man. How can you be friends with anyone if you think he might become your enemy? In such a case you would have to desire and hope that your supposed friend would do wrong as often as possible to give you things to use against him if someday he became your enemy. You would be angry, pained, and grudging every time this friend did something right.

60. Quare hoc quidem praeceptum, cuius-
cumque est, ad tollendam amicitiam valet. Illud
potius praecipiendum fuit, ut eam diligentiam
adhiberemus in amicitiis comparandis, ut ne
quando amare inciperemus eum quem aliquando
odisse possemus. Quin etiam si minus felices
in deligendo fuissemus, ferendum id Scipio po-
tius quam inimicitiarum tempus cogitandum
putabat.

61. His igitur finibus utendum arbitror, ut
cum emendati mores amicorum sint, tum sit
inter eos omnium rerum, consiliorum, volun-
tatum sine ulla exceptione communitas; ut
etiam si qua fortuna acciderit ut minus iustae
amicorum voluntates adiuvandae sint, in qui-
bus eorum aut caput agatur aut fama, declinan-
dum de via sit, modo ne summa turpitudo se-
quatur. Est enim quatenus amicitiae dari venia
possit. Nec vero neglegenda est fama, nec me-
diocre telum ad res gerendas existimare oportet

60. Therefore this precept, whoever said it, would actually have the effect of destroying friendships. A better way would be for us to take great care in forming friendships in the first place so that we don't begin to love someone we might someday hate. Scipio even thought that if it turns out we made poor choices in friends, we should stick by them rather than look for an opportunity to become enemies.

61. I think these are the boundaries we should follow in friendship: if the character of two friends is essentially faultless, then they should share with each other all actions, plans, and wishes. But if, by some chance, a friend asks us to support his inappropriate desires in matters regarding his life or reputation, we should be willing to turn aside from the straight and narrow path to help him—as long as he isn't asking for something utterly shameful. (After all, there are limits to what we should do for a friend.)

benevolentiam civium; quam blanditiis et assentando colligere turpe est: virtus, quam sequitur caritas, minime repudianda est.

62. Sed—saepe enim redeo ad Scipionem, cuius omnis sermo erat de amicitia—querebatur quod omnibus in rebus homines diligentiores essent: capras et oves quot quisque haberet dicere posse, amicos quot haberet non posse dicere; et in illis quidem parandis adhibere curam, in amicis eligendis neglegentis esse, nec habere quasi signa quaedam et notas, quibus eos qui ad amicitias essent idonei iudicarent. Sunt igitur firmi et stabiles et constantes eligendi, cuius generis est magna penuria. Et iudicare difficile est sane nisi expertum; experiendum autem est in

But we shouldn't underestimate the importance of reputation or think the goodwill of one's fellow citizens a weapon for getting things done, even if it would be shameful to acquire it for ourselves through fawning and flattery. Virtue, which draws affection, is not to be dismissed lightly.[33]

62. Scipio—I often mention him because he was always talking about friendship—used to complain that people were more careful about everything else in their lives than they were about friends. He said that everyone is able to tell you how many goats and sheep they have, but not how many friends. They take great care in acquiring the former, though not the latter. They don't even have certain signs or measures to judge who is fit to be their friend. But I think we ought to select friends who are steady, firm, and dependable—a rather small group to choose

ipsa amicitia. Ita praecurrit amicitia iudicium, tollitque experiendi potestatem.

63. Est igitur prudentis sustinere ut cursum, sic impetum benevolentiae, quo utamur quasi equis temptatis, sic amicitia ex aliqua parte periclitatis moribus amicorum. Quidam saepe in parva pecunia perspiciuntur quam sint leves; quidam autem, quos parva movere non potuit, cognoscuntur in magna. Sin vero erunt aliqui reperti qui pecuniam praeferre amicitiae sordidum existiment, ubi eos inveniemus qui honores, magistratus, imperia, potestates, opes, amicitiae non anteponant, ut cum ex altera parte proposita haec sint, ex altera ius amicitiae, non multo illa malint? Imbecilla enim est natura ad contemnendam potentiam; quam etiamsi

from nowadays. The problem is that it's difficult to determine who has the desirable qualities of a friend without trying them out—and the only way to try them out is by being their friend. Thus friendship runs ahead of judgment and removes the possibility of a trial period.

63. Therefore it is prudent to restrain a headlong rush of goodwill just as we would hold back a chariot team. As we always test horses before racing them, so in the same way we should test the character of potential friends. Some people will reveal their poor character in simple financial affairs. Others who behave well when small amounts of money are involved will reveal their true selves when large amounts are at stake. Even when we find those who would never put money above friendship, where will we find men who don't place friends below honors, political offices, military commands, power, or riches? When you put these things

neglecta amicitia consecuti sint, obscuratum iri arbitrantur, quia non sine magna causa sit neglecta amicitia.

64. Itaque verae amicitiae difficillime reperiuntur in iis qui in honoribus reque publica versantur; ubi enim istum invenias, qui honorem amici anteponat suo? Quid, haec ut omittam, quam graves, quam difficiles plerisque videntur calamitatuam societates? Ad quas non est facile inventu qui descendant. Quamquam Ennius recte 'Amicus certus in re incerta cernitur,' tamen haec duo levitatis et infirmitatis plerosque convincunt, aut si in bonis rebus contemnunt, aut in malis deserunt. Qui igitur utraque in re gravem, constantem, stabilem se in amicitia praestiterit, hunc ex maxime raro

on one side and friendship on the other, won't most people choose them over friendship? Human nature is weak when it comes to rejecting such things. Some people even think it will be overlooked if they choose power over friends, because friendship was neglected for an important reason.

64. And so true friendships are very difficult to discover among those holding political office and those in public affairs. For where would you find someone who puts a friend's advancement above his own success? And placing this consideration aside, how grievous and difficult it seems for most people to share in the misfortunes of others! It's not easy to find someone who will descend to the depths of calamity with a friend. Ennius, though, was right when he said:

A faithful friend in troubled fate is found.

genere hominum iudicare debemus et paene
divino.

65. Firmamentum autem stabilitatis constan-
tiaeque eius, quam in amicitia quaerimus, fides:
nihil est enim stabile quod infidum est. Simpli-
cem praeterea et communem et consentientem,
id est qui rebus isdem moveatur, eligi par est;
quae omnia pertinent ad fidelitatem. Neque
enim fidum potest esse multiplex ingenium et
tortuosum, neque vero qui non isdem rebus
movetur naturaque consentit aut fidus aut sta-
bilis potest esse.

Addendum eodem est ut ne criminibus aut
inferendis delectetur aut credat oblatis; quae
pertinent omnia ad eam quam iamdudum tracto

Yet most men are revealed to be weak and un-reliable when either they themselves are doing well or a friend of theirs is doing badly. If we can find someone in either situation who has proven himself reliable, constant, and firm in friendship, we should consider him the rarest kind of human being—or almost a god.

65. The foundation of stability and constancy that we seek in friendship is loyalty, for noth-ing can be stable that is disloyal. We also need to choose a friend who is honest, sociable, and sympathetic—that is, someone who is motivated by the same things as we are. All these things contribute to loyalty between people. For a character full of twists and turns cannot be loyal, nor can someone who is not moved by the same things and whose nature is fundamentally dif-ferent from yours be either loyal or steadfast.

Another factor to consider in seeking a friend who is reliable—as I've been discussing for some

constantiam. Ita fit verum illud quod initio dixi: amicitiam nisi inter bonos esse non posse.

Est enim boni viri, quem eundem sapientem licet dicere, haec duo tenere in amicitia: primum ne quid fictum sit neve simulatum (aperte enim vel odisse magis ingenui est quam fronte occultare sententiam); deinde non solum ab aliquo allatas criminationes repellere, sed ne ipsum quidem esse suspiciosum, semper aliquid existimantem ab amico esse violatum.

66. Accedat huc suavitas quaedam oportet sermonum atque morum, haudquaquam mediocre condimentum amicitiae; tristitia autem et in omni re severitas habet illa quidem gravitatem, sed amicitia remissior esse debet et liberior et dulcior et ad omnem comitatem facilitatemque proclivior.

time—is to find someone who doesn't delight in spreading rumors about you or believes such rumors when he hears them from others. For as I've said from the beginning, true friendship can't exist except between good people.

A good man—whom we also call wise— holds to these two principles of friendship: first, never to lie or deceive (for a genuine man disagrees openly with a friend rather than hiding his real thoughts); second, always to reject slander brought by another and not even to be suspicious or believe that a friend has done something wrong.

66. In addition, there should be a certain pleasantness of speech and actions between two people that gives a special flavor to friendship. Severity and seriousness are impressive in their proper place, but friendship ought to be more amiable, genial, and relaxed so that it tends toward sociability and ease of every sort.

67. Exsistit autem hoc loco quaedam quaestio subdifficilis: num quando amici novi digni amicitia veteribus sint anteponendi, ut equis vetulis teneros anteponere solemus. Indigna homine dubitatio: non enim debent esse amicitiarum, sicut aliarum rerum, satietates; veterrima quaeque, ut ea vina quae vetustatem ferunt, esse debet suavissima, verumque illud est quod dicitur, multos modios salis simul edendos esse ut amicitiae munus expletum sit.

68. Novitates autem, si spem adferunt ut tamquam in herbis non fallacibus fructus appareat, non sunt illae quidem repudiandae, vetustas tamen suo loco conservanda; maxima est enim vis vetustatis et consuetudinis. Quin in ipso equo cuius modo feci mentionem, si nulla res impediat, nemo est quin eo quo consuevit libentius utatur quam intractato et novo. Nec vero in hoc, quod est animal, sed in eis etiam

67. But at this point there is a difficult question we might ask ourselves: If we have new friends worthy of our friendship, should we prefer them to old friends, as we prefer young horses to old? What a disgraceful question for a human being! For it is impossible to be too full of friendships, as it is with other things. Like wine, an old friendship grows more delightful with time. And the saying is true that we must eat quite a few bushels of salt together before the debts of friendship are paid.

68. Of course we shouldn't cut off new friendships that look hopeful, like green shoots that promise to bear fruit; but old friendships must preserve their special place in our lives. Time and habit are powerful forces. Even with the horses just mentioned, as long as there's no problem with an animal, we would rather use one we're accustomed to rather than one unbroken and new. Familiarity is important not

quae sunt inanima consuetudo valet, cum locis
ipsis delectemur, montuosis etiam et silvestri-
bus, in quibus diutius commorati sumus.

69. Sed maximum est in amicitia parem esse
inferiori. Saepe enim excellentiae quaedam sunt,
qualis erat Scipionis in nostro (ut ita dicam)
grege. Numquam se ille Philo, numquam
Rupilio, numquam Mummio anteposuit, num-
quam inferioris ordinis amicis; Quintum vero
Maximum fratrem, egregium virum omnino,
sibi nequaquam parem, quod is anteibat aetate,
tamquam superiorem colebat; suosque omnes
per se ipsos esse ampliores volebat.

70. Quod faciendum imitandumque est om-
nibus, ut si quam praestantiam virtutis ingenii
fortunae consecuti sint, impertiant ea suis
communicentque cum proximis; ut si parenti-
bus nati sint humilibus, si propinquos habeant

just with living things but with inanimate as well, such as places we delight in and have spent time in even if they're rugged and wild.

69. It is especially important to treat friends of a lower rank as equals. Often in friendships one person will stand out above the others, as Scipio did in what I would call our little flock. But never did he treat Philus or Rupilius or Mummius or any of his friends of inferior rank as less important than himself.[34] Even his brother Quintus Maximus—a fine fellow in his own way, though not equal to Scipio—he held as his superior because he was older. Scipio also always tried to improve the prospects of his friends by his association with him.

70. This is an example we should all follow, so that if you have an advantage in virtue or talent or fortune, you should share it freely with your family and those you are close to. For example, if your parents are of humble birth or

imbecilliore vel animo vel fortuna, eorum augeant opes eisque honori sint et dignitati; ut in
fabulis, qui aliquamdiu propter ignorationem
stirpis et generis in famulatu fuerunt, cum cogniti sunt et aut deorum aut regum filii inventi,
retinent tamen caritatem in pastores quos patres
multos annos esse duxerunt. Quod est multo
profecto magis in veris patribus certisque faciendum; fructus enim ingeni et virtutis omnisque praestantiae tum maximus capitur, cum in
proximum quemque confertur.

71. Ut igitur ei qui sunt in amicitiae coniunctionisque necessitudine superiores exaequare
se cum inferioribus debent, sic inferiores non
dolere se a suis aut ingenio aut fortuna aut dignitate superari. Quorum plerique aut queruntur semper aliquid aut etiam exprobrant, eoque

your relatives are not as gifted as you are in brains, energy, or fortune, you should increase their resources and improve their honor and standing in life. Do you remember those stories where characters unaware of their noble parents and true birth served for years as slaves? When they at last discover that they're really the children of gods or kings, they still love the humble shepherds they thought for years were their parents. So surely for us the debt we owe to our real and certain parents is even greater. For the fruit of talent, virtue, or any other excellence we might have is best enjoyed when we share it with those nearest and dearest to us.

71. Therefore, just as friends and acquaintances who are superior should put themselves on a level with those who are lacking, so those who are inferior should not be hurt if their friends surpass them in talent or money or standing. Too many of the latter are forever

magis si habere se putant, quod officiose et amice
et cum labore aliquo suo factum queant dicere:
odiosum sane genus hominum, officia expro-
brantium, quae meminisse debet is in quem
collata sunt, non commemorare qui contulit.

72. Quam ob rem ut ii qui superiores sunt
submittere se debent in amicitia, sic quodam
modo inferiores extollere. Sunt enim quidam
qui molestas amicitias faciunt cum ipsi se con-
temni putant; quod non fere contingit nisi eis
qui etiam contemnendos se arbitrantur; qui hac
opinione non modo verbis sed etiam opere le-
vandi sunt.

73. Tantum autem cuique tribuendum, pri-
mum quantum ipse efficere possis, deinde
etiam quantum ille, quem diligas atque adiuves,

whining and complaining, especially if they think that they have done some job or favor for a friend that required some great effort on their part. Such people are so tiresome. It's up to the one who received the favor to remember the kindness and be grateful, not the one who did the service to remind him.

72. As I have said, someone who is superior ought to bring himself down to the level of his friends and try to raise them up when he can. Some people turn friendship into an annoyance by thinking they are being treated with a lack of respect—something which rarely happens except when a person actually deserves it! But we should try to relieve such friends of their misconception not only with words but by our actions as well.

73. You should, first of all, give as much help to each friend as you are able. But on the other hand, you should only give them what they can

sustinere. Non enim neque tu possis, quamvis
excellas, omnes tuos ad honores amplissimos
perducere; ut Scipio P. Rupilium potuit con-
sulem efficere, fratrem eius Lucium non potuit.
Quod si etiam possis quidvis deferre ad alterum,
videndum est tamen, quid ille possit sustinere.

74. Omnino amicitiae corroboratis iam con-
firmatisque et ingeniis et aetatibus iudicandae
sunt; nec si qui ineunte aetate venandi aut pilae
studiosi fuerunt, eos habere necessarios quos
tum eodem studio praeditos dilexerunt. Isto
enim modo nutrices et paedagogi iure vetus-
tatis plurimum benevolentiae postulabunt; qui
neglegendi quidem non sunt, sed alio quodam
modo <* * *> Aliter amicitiae stabiles perma-
nere non possunt; dispares enim mores disparia
studia sequuntur, quorum dissimilitudo disso-
ciat amicitias; nec ob aliam causam ullam boni
improbis, improbi bonis amici esse non possunt,

handle. No matter how successful you are, you cannot help all your friends rise to the top. Scipio was able to help Publius Rupilius become consul, but he couldn't do the same for his brother Lucius. So even if you can do a great deal for your friends, you have to always consider how much help would do them any good.

74. As a general rule we shouldn't commit to friendships until we've reached an age when our character and way of living are established and confirmed. If someone was fond of hunting and playing ball with other boys when he was young, that doesn't mean he'll keep those childhood companions as friends when he grows up. If such a principle held true, our nursemaids and family slaves would have the greatest claim on our friendship since they've known us the longest. Of course, such servants shouldn't be neglected, but they should be thought of in a very different way. Waiting

nisi quod tanta est inter eos quanta maxima
potest esse morum studiorumque distantia.

75. Recte etiam praecipi potest in amicitiis,
ne intemperata quaedam benevolentia, quod
persaepe fit, impediat magnas utilitates amico-
rum. Nec enim, ut ad fabulas redeam, Troiam
Neoptolemus capere potuisset, si Lycomedem,
apud quem erat educatus, multis cum lacrimis
iter suum impedientem audire voluisset. Et saepe
incidunt magnae res, ut discedendum sit ab am-
icis; quas qui impedire vult eo quod desiderium
non facile ferat, is et infirmus est mollisque na-
tura et ob eam ipsam causam in amicitia parum
iustus.

until we are adults is the only way to form stable friendships. Different characters spring from different interests—and this disparity is what tears friendships apart. This is the whole reason good people can't be friends with bad or bad with good. Their characters and interests are simply too different.

75. Another important rule of friendship is that we not let an excess of affection—as often happens—prevent someone from pursuing a worthwhile opportunity to be useful to others. To draw an example from an ancient story, Neoptolemus [the son of Achilles] would never have conquered Troy if he had listened to his grandfather Lycomedes who had raised him and tried with many tears to prevent him from leaving home. Often important tasks compel us to be apart from our friends. Anyone who tries to prevent you from following through on a great opportunity because he can't manage his

76. Atque in omni re considerandum est et quid postules ab amico, et quid patiare a te impetrari.

Est etiam quaedam calamitas in amicitiis dimittendis non numquam necessaria (iam enim a sapientium familiaritatibus ad vulgares amicitias oratio nostra delabitur). Erumpunt saepe vitia amicorum, tum in ipsos amicos, tum in alienos, quorum tamen ad amicos redundet infamia. Tales igitur amicitiae sunt remissione usus eluendae, et ut Catonem dicere audivi, dissuendae magis quam discindendae, nisi quaedam admodum intolerabilis iniuria exarserit, ut neque rectum neque honestum sit nec fieri possit ut non statim alienatio disiunctioque faciunda sit.

own sorrow at your absence is weak and unmanly by nature—and that is precisely what causes him to be unreasonable in friendship.

76. You should always consider what is right for you to ask of a friend—and what is right for that friend to ask of you.

There is sometimes unavoidable disaster when we break off a friendship—and I'm speaking now of common, everyday friendships, not those among wise people. Often among such friends one will display vices that affect his friends or others. In this way that man's bad reputation begins to spread to his friends as well as himself. In these cases you should loosen your connections to that person—or, as I hear Cato put it, the ties of friendship should be unraveled rather than cut. Sadly though there are times when a friend's actions are so reprehensible that honor demands the friendship be ended immediately and publicly.

77. Sin autem aut morum aut studiorum commutatio quaedam, ut fieri solet, facta erit, aut in rei publicae partibus dissensio intercesserit (loquor enim iam, ut paulo ante dixi, non de sapientium, sed de communibus amicitiis), cavendum erit ne non solum amicitiae depositae, sed etiam inimicitiae susceptae videantur. Nihil est enim turpius quam cum eo bellum gerere quocum familiariter vixeris. Ab amicitia Q. Pompei meo nomine se removerat, ut scitis, Scipio; propter dissensionem autem quae erat in re publica, alienatus est a collega nostro Metello; utrumque egit graviter, ac moderate et offensione animi non acerba.

78. Quam ob rem primum danda opera est ne qua amicorum discidia fiant; sin tale aliquid evenerit, ut exstinctae potius amicitiae quam oppressae videantur. Cavendum vero ne etiam in graves inimicitias convertant se amicitiae, ex

77. But if, as more commonly happens between friends, there is a change in character or interests or political views—I'm speaking, as I just said, of ordinary friendships, not those between the wise—we must take care that those who were once our friends don't become our enemies. For nothing is more disgraceful than to wage war against someone you once loved. As you both know, Scipio ended his friendship with Quintus Pompeius on my account. He also became estranged from my colleague Metellus because of a political disagreement.[35] But he handled both occasions with gravity and moderation, and without any bitter resentment of spirit.

78. So first make a great effort to see that discord doesn't arise between you and your friends. But if it does, make it seem that the fire of your friendship burned out on its own rather than being stamped out. Again, make sure these

quibus iurgia maledicta contumeliae gignuntur.
Quae tamen si tolerabiles erunt, ferendae sunt,
et hic honos veteri amicitiae tribuendus, ut is in
culpa sit qui faciat, non is qui patiatur iniuriam.
Omnino omnium horum vitiorum atque in-
commodorum una cautio est atque una provi-
sio, ut ne nimis cito diligere incipiant, neve non
dignos.

79. Digni autem sunt amicitia quibus in ipsis
est causa cur diligantur; rarum genus, et quidem
omnia praeclara rara, nec quidquam difficilius
quam reperire quod sit omni ex parte in suo ge-
nere perfectum.

Sed plerique neque in rebus humanis quid-
quam bonum norunt, nisi quod fructuosum sit,
et amicos, tamquam pecudes, eos potissimum
diligunt ex quibus sperant se maximum fruc-
tum esse capturos.

former friends don't turn into bitter enemies, for that's how slander, accusations, and back-biting start. But you should endure even these for the sake of honor paid to your former friend-ship. Let people say the other person is behaving badly and not you.

There is only one way to prevent such un-pleasantness and that is to make sure in the first place that you don't love too quickly and don't give your friendship to those unworthy of it.

79. Those worthy to be your friends are those who have within themselves reasons to be loved — a rare type, but then everything precious is rare. Nothing is harder than to find something that's a perfect specimen of its kind in every way.

The majority of people in this world see nothing good in anyone unless that person can somehow profit them—as if they were buying cattle! They value a person the most who can give them the best return on their investment.

80. Ita pulcherrima illa et maxime naturali carent amicitia, per se et propter se expetita, nec ipsi sibi exemplo sunt, haec vis amicitiae et qualis et quanta sit. Ipse enim se quisque diligit, non ut aliquam a se ipse mercedem exigat caritatis suae, sed quod per se sibi quisque carus est; quod nisi idem in amicitiam transferetur, verus amicus numquam reperietur; est enim is qui est tamquam alter idem.

81. Quod si hoc apparet in bestiis, volucribus nantibus agrestibus, cicuribus feris, primum ut se ipsae diligant (id enim pariter cum omni animante nascitur), deinde ut requirant atque appetant ad quas se applicent eiusdem generis animantis, idque faciunt cum desiderio et cum quadam similitudine amoris humani, quanto id magis in homine fit natura, qui et se ipse diligit, et alterum anquirit cuius animum

80. In this way such people neglect the most beautiful and natural kind of friendship, the one sought in and for itself. Nor do they have any idea from their own experience how powerful this type of friendship can be. For every person loves himself, not for any kind of profit he can make from this love but because he is dear to himself on his own account. Unless we can transfer this kind of feeling to friendship, we will never find true friendship. A friend is, quite simply, another self.

81. It's obvious that even animals—whether of the air, water, or land, be they tame or wild—first love themselves. This feeling is in every creature equally from birth. It's also obvious that they need and seek after creatures like themselves to be with. This longing in animals is almost like human love. But how much more does nature cause this to happen for a human being, who both loves himself and seeks another

ita cum suo misceat ut efficiat paene unum ex duobus.

82. Sed plerique perverse, ne dicam impudenter, habere talem amicum volunt quales ipsi esse non possunt, quaeque ipsi non tribuunt amicis, haec ab iis desiderant. Par est autem primum ipsum esse virum bonum, tum alterum similem sui quaerere. In talibus, ea quam iam dudum tractamus stabilitas amicitiae confirmari potest, cum homines benevolentia coniuncti primum cupiditatibus eis quibus ceteri serviunt imperabunt, deinde aequitate iustitiaque gaudebunt, omniaque alter pro altero suscipiet, neque quidquam umquam nisi honestum et rectum alter ab altero postulabit; neque solum colent inter se et diligent, sed etiam verebuntur; nam maximum ornamentum amicitiae tollit qui ex ea tollit verecundiam.

soul to mix with his own in such a way that the two almost become one!

82. But most people have a foolish and perverse idea that friends should have the qualities they themselves lack. These people seek from friendship what they themselves cannot give. It's right, however, first of all to be a good person yourself, and then to seek someone similar to you. With people like this, it's much easier to have the sort of stable friendship I've been talking about. When such people are united in goodwill, they will first conquer the desires that enslave other people, then delight in what is just and fair, and go to any lengths for each other. They will never ask from the other anything but what is honorable and right. They will not only cherish and love but also respect one another. For whoever takes away respect from a friendship takes away its most precious jewel.

83. Itaque in eis perniciosus est error, qui existimant libidinum peccatorumque omnium patere in amicitia licentiam. Virtutum amicitia adiutrix a natura data est, non vitiorum comes; ut quoniam solitaria non posset virtus ad ea quae summa sunt pervenire, coniuncta et consociata cum altera perveniret. Quae si quos inter societas aut est aut fuit aut futura est, eorum est habendus ad summum naturae bonum optumus beatissimusque comitatus.

84. Haec est, inquam, societas, in qua omnia insunt quae putant homines expetenda—honestas, gloria, tranquillitas animi atque iucunditas—ut et cum haec adsint, beata vita sit, et sine his esse non possit. Quod cum optimum maximumque sit, si id volumus adipisci, virtuti opera danda est, sine qua nec amicitiam neque ullam rem expetendam consequi possumus. Ea vero neglecta qui se amicos habere arbitrantur,

83. It is a terrible mistake to think that friendship provides us with a license for wicked passions and every sort of wrongdoing. Nature gave us friendship as an aide to virtue, not as a companion to vice. Virtue isn't able to attain its highest goals when we are alone, but only when we are joined and bound to someone else. This sort of relationship—whether it was or is or will be—should be considered the best and most blessed company on the journey to nature's highest good.

84. In this kind of relationship we find everything that people think worthwhile—honor, glory, and the tranquility and joy of our souls. When we possess these things, life is happy. When we don't, it cannot be. Happiness is the greatest and highest good, so if we want to achieve it, we must devote ourselves to striving after virtue. For without it, we won't be able to find friendship or any other desirable thing.

tum se denique errasse sentiunt, cum eos gravis aliquis casus experiri cogit.

85. Quocirca (dicendum est enim saepius) cum iudicaris diligere oportet, non cum dilexeris iudicare. Sed cum multis in rebus neglegentia plectimur, tum maxime in amicis et diligendis et colendis; praeposteris enim utimur consiliis, et acta agimus, quod vetamur vetere proverbio; nam implicati ultro et citro vel usu diuturno vel etiam officiis, repente in medio cursu amicitias, exorta aliqua offensione, disrumpimus.

86. Quo etiam magis vituperanda est rei maxime necessariae tanta incuria: una est enim amicitia in rebus humanis de cuius utilitate

Those who lack virtue but believe they have friends are in for a grave disappointment when some tragedy strikes and these supposed friends are put to the test.

85. And so—it can't be repeated often enough—you should love after you have judged, not judge after you have loved. We pay the price for negligence in many things, but most of all for our carelessness in selecting and making friends. We often deliberate after acting, violating the ancient proverb that we shouldn't argue a case after the verdict has been rendered. In this way, after we've been bound to some friend by long association or mutual favors, we have to break off that friendship in the middle of its course because an unanticipated offense occurs.

86. Our carelessness regarding something as important as friendship deserves the strongest condemnation, for it is the one thing in human

omnes uno ore consentiunt. quamquam a multis virtus ipsa contemnitur, et venditatio quaedam atque ostentatio esse dicitur; multi divitias despiciunt, quos parvo contentos tenuis victus cultusque delectat; honores vero, quorum cupiditate quidam inflammantur, quam multi ita contemnunt ut nihil inanius, nihil esse levius existiment! Itemque cetera quae quibusdam admirabilia videntur, permulti sunt qui pro nihilo putent; de amicitia omnes ad unum idem sentiunt, et ei qui ad rem publicam se contulerunt, et ei qui rerum cognitione doctrinaque delectantur, et ei qui suum negotium gerunt otiosi, postremo ei qui se totos tradiderunt voluptatibus: sine amicitia vitam esse nullam, si modo velint aliqua ex parte liberaliter vivere.

87. Serpit enim nescioquo modo per omnium vitas amicitia, nec ullam aetatis degendae rationem patitur esse expertem sui. Quin etiam si

life that everyone unanimously agrees is useful. Some people spurn the idea of virtue and see it as nothing more than pretense and self-promotion. Others despise riches and delight in meager food and tattered clothing. And the pursuit of honors that captivates some is condemned by others as frivolous and inane. Anything that one group of people thinks admirable another will consider worthless—but about friendship, every single person feels the same way. Those who devote themselves to politics, those who delight in learning and philosophy, those who conduct their business apart from public concerns, those who have given themselves entirely to pleasure—all agree that a life without friendship is no life at all, unless they want to live like slaves.

87. One way or another, friendship creeps into every life and allows no way of living without it. Even a person so savage and fierce by

quis asperitate ea est et immanitate naturae,
congressus ut hominum fugiat atque oderit,
qualem fuisse Athenis Timonem nescioquem
accepimus, tamen is pati non possit ut non an-
quirat aliquem apud quem evomat virus acerbi-
tatis suae. Atque hoc maxime iudicaretur si quid
tale posset contingere, ut aliquis nos deus ex hac
hominum frequentia tolleret et in solitudine
uspiam collocaret, atque ibi suppeditans om-
nium rerum quas natura desiderat abundantiam
et copiam, hominis omnino aspiciendi potes-
tatem eriperet. Quis tam esset ferreus, qui eam
vitam ferre posset, cuique non auferret fructum
voluptatum omnium solitudo?

88. Verum ergo illud est, quod a Tarentino
Archyta, ut opinor, dici solitum nostros senes
commemorare audivi, ab aliis senibus audi-
tum: si quis in caelum ascendisset, naturamque
mundi et pulchritudinem siderum perspexis-
set, insuavem illam admirationem ei fore, quae

nature that he shuns and loathes human society, like the legendary Timon of Athens, can't stand not to have someone around him on whom to spew his poison.[36] Judge by the following whether or not I'm right: Suppose a god carried you far away to a place where you were granted an abundance of every material good nature could wish for, but denied the possibility of ever seeing a human being. Wouldn't you have to be as hard as iron to endure that sort of life? Wouldn't you, utterly alone, lose every capacity for joy and pleasure?

88. It's true what that man said, Archytas of Tarentum I believe. I've heard old men say it who heard it from other old men before them.[37] He said that if someone were to ascend into the heavens and gaze at the nature of the universe and the beauty of the stars, that very wonder

iucundissima fuisset si aliquem cui narraret habuisset. Sic natura solitarium nihil amat, semperque ad aliquod tamquam adminiculum adnititur, quod in amicissimo quoque dulcissimum est.

Sed cum tot signis eadem natura declaret quid velit, anquirat, desideret, tamen obsurdescimus nescio quo modo, nec ea quae ab ea monemur audimus. Est enim varius et multiplex usus amicitiae, multaeque causae suspicionum offensionumque dantur; quas tum evitare, tum elevare, tum ferre sapientis est. Una illa sublevanda offensio est, ut et utilitas in amicitia et fides retineatur; nam et monendi amici saepe sunt et obiurgandi, et haec accipienda amice cum benevole fiunt.

89. Sed nescioquo modo verum est quod in Andria familiaris meus dicit: 'Obsequium

would be bitter for him, which would be the most delightful of all if he had someone to tell. Nature loves nothing that is solitary, but always inclines toward some sort of support. And the sweetest support is a very dear friend.

Although nature shows us through so many signs what it is she wants, seeks, and longs for, yet somehow we have grown deaf and do not hear her voice. Friendship has many and various advantages, but it also offers many opportunities for suspicion and offense. The latter, if we are wise, we should sometimes avoid, sometimes laugh off, and sometimes endure. And one occasion for offense we must learn to accept if we want a friendship that is useful and trustworthy is listening to the advice and criticism of a friend when given in a spirit of goodwill.

89. What my friend [Terence the comic playwright] says in his *Andrian Girl* is somehow

amicos, veritas odium parit.' Molesta veritas,
siquidem ex ea nascitur odium, quod est vene-
num amicitiae; sed obsequium multo moles-
tius, quod peccatis indulgens praecipitem am-
icum ferri sinit; maxima autem culpa in eo qui
et veritatem aspernatur et in fraudem obsequio
impellitur. Omni igitur hac in re habenda ratio
et diligentia est, primum ut monitio acerbi-
tate, deinde ut obiurgatio contumelia careat; in
obsequio autem (quoniam Terentiano verbo
libenter utimur) comitas adsit, assentatio, vitio-
rum adiutrix procul amoveatur, quae non modo
amico, sed ne libero quidem digna est; aliter
enim cum tyranno, aliter cum amico vivitur.

90. Cuius autem aures clausae veritati sunt,
ut ab amico verum audire nequeat, huius salus
desperanda est. Scitum est enim illud Catonis,
ut multa: melius de quibusdam acerbos inimicos

true: "Indulgence gets us friends, but truth gets us hatred."[38] Truth can indeed be troublesome if it brings about hatred, which is poison to friendship; but much worse is the kind of indulgence and acquiescence that allows a friend to rush headlong into destructive behavior. However, the worst sin of all is to spurn the truth and allow flattery to drive you to ruin. And so we all must use reason and care to advise our friends without harshness and chasten them without insult. If we indulge a friend, to use Terence's term, we should do so with courtesy, and keep flattery, that handmaid of vice, at a distance. For flattery is unworthy not only of a friend, but of any free person; living with a friend should not be like living with a tyrant.

90. Of course, if a person's ears are so closed that he won't even hear the truth from a friend, he is a lost cause. Cato was right about this, as about so many things: "Some people's most

mereri quam eos amicos qui dulces videantur; illos verum saepe dicere, hos numquam. Atque illud absurdum, quod ei qui monentur eam molestiam quam debent capere non capiunt, eam capiunt qua debent vacare; peccasse enim se non anguntur, obiurgari moleste ferunt; quod contra oportebat delicto dolere, correctione gaudere.

91. Ut igitur et monere et moneri proprium est verae amicitiae, et alterum libere facere, non aspere, alterum patienter accipere, non repugnanter, sic habendum est nullam in amicitiis pestem esse maiorem quam adulationem, blanditiam, assentationem; quamvis enim multis nominibus est hoc vitium notandum, levium hominum atque fallacium, ad voluntatem loquentium omnia, nihil ad veritatem.

bitter enemies are more helpful to them than their sweet-seeming friends, since the former often tell the truth but the latter never do." It's absurd that when people receive advice they aren't bothered by what they should be, but are bothered by what they shouldn't be: they aren't upset because they've done wrong, but because they're being criticized! They ought to do the opposite, grieving at the fault and rejoicing at the correction.

91. To graciously give and receive criticism is the mark of true friendship. You must offer your corrections with kindness, not harshly, and take them patiently, not with reluctance. Nothing is worse or more destructive among friends than constant flattery, fawning, and affirmation. Call it what you will, it is the mark of a weak and false-hearted man to tell you anything to please you except the truth.

92. Cum autem omnium rerum simulatio vitiosa est—tollit enim iudicium veri idque adulterat—tum amicitiae repugnat maxime; delet enim veritatem, sine qua nomen amicitiae valere non potest. Nam cum amicitiae vis sit in eo ut unus quasi animus fiat ex pluribus, qui id fieri poterit si ne in uno quidem quoque unus animus erit idemque semper, sed varius commutabilis, multiplex?

93. Quid enim potest esse tam flexibile, tam devium, quam animus eius qui ad alterius non modo sensum ac voluntatem, sed etiam vultum atque nutum convertitur?

Negat quis, nego; ait, aio; postremo imperavi egomet mihi
Omnia adsentari,

92. Hypocrisy—which blurs and corrupts our ability to decide what is true—is a despicable thing under any circumstances, but especially in friendship. It destroys truth, without which the word "friendship" is meaningless. The power of friendship is that it makes, as it were, several souls into one. How is such a union possible if even within a single person the soul does not remain constant, but instead is always shifting, changing, and divided?

93. Can there be anything more pliant, more erratic, than the soul of someone who changes not only with a friend's shifting mood and wishes but even with his expressions and nods?

He says no, so I say no; He says yes and I do
   too.
As I told myself,
just agree with him in everything.

ut ait idem Terentius, sed ille in Gnathonis persona. Quod amici genus adhibere omnino levitatis est.

94. Multi autem Gnathonum similes cum sint loco fortuna fama superiores, horum est assentatio molesta cum ad vanitatem accessit auctoritas.

95. Secerni autem blandus amicus a vero et internosci, tam potest adhibita diligentia quam omnia fucata et simulata a sinceris atque veris. Contio, quae ex imperitissimis constat, tamen iudicare solet quid intersit inter popularem, id est assentatorem et levem civem, et inter constantem et severum gravem.

96. Quibus blanditiis C. Papirius nuper influebat in auris contionis, cum ferret legem de tribunis plebis reficiendis! Dissuasimus nos, sed nihil de me; de Scipione dicam libentius; quanta

That's Terence again, but this time speaking in the character Gnatho.[39] To offer friendship of this sort is a complete joke.

94. But there are many such people like Gnatho who are of higher rank, fortune, and reputation. These distinguished men thus lend a dangerous authority to their flattery.

95. However, with careful attention, it is possible to distinguish a flattering friend from a true one, just as with diligence we can separate something false and pretended from something genuine and true. Public assemblies, which are full of uneducated men, can still more often than not are able to tell the difference between a shallow, pandering demagogue and a man who is steady, sincere, and responsible.

96. What flattery Gaius Papirius poured into the ears of the assembly recently when he proposed a law allowing tribunes of the people to be re-elected![40] I was against it, of course, but

illa, di immortales, fuit gravitas, quanta in ora-
tione maiestas, ut facile ducem populi Romani,
non comitem diceres! Sed adfuistis et est in
manibus oratio. Itaque lex popularis suffragiis
populi repudiata est. Atque ut ad me redeam,
meministis, Q. Maximo fratre Scipionis et L.
Mancino consulibus, quam popularis lex de sac-
erdotiis C. Licini Crassi videbatur; cooptatio
enim collegiorum ad populi beneficium trans-
ferebatur; atque is primus instituit in forum
versus agere cum populo; tamen illius vend-
ibilem orationem religio deorum immortalium,
nobis defendentibus, facile vincebat. Atque id
actum est praetore me, quinquennio ante quam
consul sum factus; ita re magis quam summa
auctoritate causa illa defensa est.

I'm really not one to talk about myself. I'd prefer to speak of Scipio. But immortal gods, there was such gravity and majesty in the speech of Papirius! You would have easily said he was the leader of the Roman people, not just their comrade. (You both were there, and the speech is published, so I won't dwell on it.) As a result, this supposed law of the people was soundly defeated by the people's votes.

Forgive me if I speak of myself once more, but you remember, when Scipio's brother Quintus Maximus and Lucius Mancinus were consuls, how popular that law regarding priestly offices proposed by Gaius Licinius Crassus seemed.[41] He wanted vacancies to be filled by a vote of the assembly. (By the way, Crassus was the first one to face the forum while addressing the people.) Nevertheless, when I argued against this bill, respect for the immortal gods easily prevailed over his shameless flattery. And

97. Quod si in scaena, id est in contione, in qua rebus fictis et adumbratis loci plurimum est, tamen verum valet, si modo id patefactum et illustratum est, quid in amicitia fieri oportet, quae tota veritate perpenditur? In qua nisi, ut dicitur, apertum pectus videas tuumque ostendas, nihil fidum, nihil exploratum habeas, ne amare quidem aut amari, cum id quam vere fiat, ignores.

Quamquam ista assentatio, quamvis perniciosa sit, nocere tamen nemini potest nisi ei qui eam recipit atque ea delectatur. Ita fit, ut is assentatoribus patefaciat aures suas maxime, qui ipse sibi assentetur et se maxime ipse delectet.

at the time I was only a praetor, five years before my election as consul, so you can see that my arguments persuaded the crowd on their own merit, not because I commanded any great authority.

97. Now if truth—once made clear and brought into the light of day—prevails on the political stage with all its lying and deceit, how much more important is it in friendship which depends on it entirely? In friendship, as they say, unless you see an open heart and reveal your own, you'll have nothing certain or trustworthy. You won't know the pleasure of truly loving or being loved, since you won't know what true love is.

But however dangerous flattery is, it can be harmful only to those who welcome and embrace it. Thus it happens that the person whose ears are most open to flatterers is the one who most gladly flatters and delights in himself.

98. Omnino est amans sui virtus, optime enim se ipsa novit, quamque amabilis sit intellegit. ego autem non de virtute nunc loquor, sed de virtutis opinione. Virtute enim ipsa non tam multi praediti esse quam videri volunt; hos delectat assentatio, his fictus ad ipsorum voluntatem sermo cum adhibetur, orationem illam vanam testimonium esse laudum suarum putant. Nulla est igitur haec amicitia, cum alter verum audire non vult, alter ad mentiendum paratus est. Nec parasitorum in comoediis assentatio faceta nobis videretur, nisi essent milites gloriosi. 'Magnas vero agere gratias Thais mihi?': satis erat respondere: 'Magnas'; 'Ingentes,' inquit. Semper auget assentator id quod is cuius ad voluntatem dicitur vult esse magnum.

98. Of course, virtue, too, loves itself, for it best understands itself and knows how lovable it is. However, I'm not speaking here of genuine virtue, but of the reputation for virtue. Not nearly as many people wish to possess virtue as to be seen to possess it; these delight in flattery, and when a phony speech is made to flatter them, they willingly take this empty display as firm proof of their own merits. Therefore such a friendship is nothing, since one person refuses to hear the truth, while the other is eager to lie. We wouldn't get to laugh at the fawning yes-men in comedies, if it weren't for the braggart soldiers. "Does Thais really send me great thanks?" [asks the soldier Thraso on stage.][42] It would be enough to reply, "Great indeed," but instead [his toady] says, "Yes, *tremendous* thanks." And so the flatterer always amplifies his response to fit what his patron wants to hear.

99. Quam ob rem quamquam blanda ista vanitas apud eos valet qui ipsi illam allectant et invitant, tamen etiam graviores constantioresque admonendi sunt ut animadvertant, ne callida assentatione capiantur. Aperte enim adulantem nemo non videt nisi qui admodum est excors; callidus ille et occultus ne se insinuet studiose cavendum est; nec enim facillime agnoscitur, quippe qui etiam adversando saepe assentetur, et litigare se simulans blandiatur atque ad extremum det manus vincique se patiatur, ut is qui illusus sit plus vidisse videatur. Quid autem turpius quam illudi? Quod ut ne accidat magis cavendum est.

Ut me hodie ante omnes comicos stultos senes
Versaris atque inlusseris lautissume—

99. Therefore, though this sort of empty flattery works best on those who are eager for it and welcome it, nevertheless, even serious and steady people must be warned to be careful not to be taken in by a more deceptive kind of lie. No one apart from an utter fool fails to recognize an obvious flatterer, but it takes special caution not to let that more skilled and subtle sort worm his way in. He's very hard to recognize, for he will often flatter you even by disagreeing with you, and lure you in by picking a quarrel, until at last he lets himself be won over—so that you, the dupe, are made to look like the one with superior insight! What could be more shameful than to be duped like this? Take special care that this doesn't happen to you, so you don't have to say:[43]

You've made me the biggest fool among old
comic actors,

100. Haec enim etiam in fabulis stultissima persona est, improvidorum et credulorum senum.

Sed nescioquo pacto ab amicitiis perfectorum hominum, id est sapientium (de hac dico sapientia, quae videtur in hominem cadere posse), ad leves amicitias defluxit oratio; quam ob rem ad illa prima redeamus eaque ipsa concludamus aliquando.

Virtus, virtus inquam, Gai Fanni et tu Quinte Muci, et conciliat amicitias et conservat. In ea est enim convenientia rerum, in ea stabilitas, in ea constantia. Quae cum se extulit et ostendit suum lumen, et idem aspexit agnovitque in alio, ad id se admovet vicissimque accipit illud quod in altero est; ex quo exardescit sive amor sive amicitia (utrumque enim dictum est ab amando);

and turned me into a chump with consummate skill.

100. The witless and gullible old man is always the most ridiculous character on the stage.

But somehow I've drifted away from the topic of friendship among good people, which is to say, wise people (I mean with the kind of "wisdom" that is possible for real people), into a discussion of frivolous friendships. So let's get back to the topic I began with and bring our discussion to an end.

Virtue—my dear Gaius Fannius and you Quintus Mucius—I say it is virtue that creates and preserves friendships. Virtue is the source of compatibility, stability, and permanence. When virtue has raised itself up and shown its light and has seen the same light in someone else, it is drawn to that person and receives what it gives another. From this sharing either love

amare autem nihil est aliud nisi eum ipsum dil-
igere quem ames nulla indigentia, nulla utilitate
quaesita, quae tamen ipsa efflorescit ex amicitia
etiamsi tu eam minus secutus sis.

101. Hac nos adulescentes benevolentia senes
illos, L. Paulum, M. Catonem, C. Galum, P.
Nasicam, Ti. Gracchum, Scipionis nostri soce-
rum, dileximus; haec etiam magis elucet inter
aequales, ut inter me et Scipionem, L. Furium,
P. Rupilium, Sp. Mummium. Vicissim autem
senes in adulescentium caritate acquiescimus,
ut in vestra, ut in Q. Tuberonis; equidem etiam
admodum adulescentis P. Rutili, A. Vergini fa-
miliaritate delector. Quoniamque ita ratio com-
parata est vitae naturaeque nostrae, ut alia ex
alia aetas oriatur, maxime quidem optandum est
ut cum aequalibus possis, quibuscum tamquam

[*amor*] or friendship [*amicitia*] shines forth, for they both come from the same word [*amare*]. To love someone simply means that you care for another person without putting your own needs or advantage first. Yet this blossoms in friendship anyway, even though you weren't actively pursuing it.

101. It was with this sort of goodwill that, when I was a young man, I felt affection for older men such as Lucius Paulus, Marcus Cato, Gaius Galus, Publius Nasica, and Tiberius Gracchus, father-in-law to my dear Scipio.[44] And although friendship shines more brightly between people of the same age—such as among Scipio, Lucius Furius, Publius Rupilius, Spurius Mummius, and myself—I find that I very much enjoy the company of younger men as well, as with you two and Quintus Tubero, but also with even younger men like Publius Rutilius and Aulus Verginius.[45] Since it's a law of

e carceribus emissus sis, cum eisdem ad calcem, ut dicitur, pervenire.

102. Sed quoniam res humanae fragiles caducaeque sunt, semper aliqui anquirendi sunt quos diligamus et a quibus diligamur. Caritate enim benevolentiaque sublata omnis est e vita sublata iucunditas.

Mihi quidem Scipio, quamquam est subito ereptus, vivit tamen semperque vivet. Virtutem enim amavi illius viri, quae exstincta non est, nec mihi soli versatur ante oculos, qui illam semper in manibus habui, sed etiam posteris erit clara et insignis. Nemo umquam animo aut spe maiora suscipiet, qui sibi non illius memoriam atque imaginem proponendam putet.

human life and human nature that a new generation is always coming forth to replace the older, it is most gratifying to complete the race of life, so to speak, together with the same people who were there with you at the starting gate.

102. But since human affairs are fragile and fleeting, we should always be seeking someone to love and to be loved by in return. For if affection and goodwill disappear from life, so does all joy.

Indeed, for me, although Scipio was snatched away suddenly, nevertheless he lives and always will live. For it was his virtue that I loved—and that has not died. Not for me alone is it constantly before my eyes—I who always had it within my reach—but it will shine bright and clear for those not yet born. No one will ever undertake the weighty tasks of life with courage and hope without thinking that he should

103. Equidem ex omnibus rebus quas mihi aut fortuna aut natura tribuit, nihil habeo quod cum amicitia Scipionis possim comparare; in hac mihi de re publica consensus, in hac rerum privatarum consilium, in eadem requies plena oblectationis fuit. Numquam illum ne minima quidem re offendi, quod quidem senserim; nihil audivi ex eo ipse quod nollem. Una domus erat, idem victus isque communis, neque solum militia, sed etiam peregrinationes rusticationesque communes.

104. Nam quid ego de studiis dicam cognoscendi semper aliquid atque discendi, in quibus remoti ab oculis populi omne otiosum tempus contrivimus? Quarum rerum recordatio et memoria si una cum illo occidisset, desiderium coniunctissimi atque amantissimi viri ferre nullo

keep before him the memory and image of that great man.

103. For my part, of all the blessings either fortune or nature has given me, there is nothing I can compare to my friendship with Scipio. In this friendship lay agreement in public affairs, wise advice in private matters, and recreation that was full of delight. As far as I know, I never offended him in even the smallest matter, nor did I ever hear a word from him I wish I hadn't. We shared one home and one way of living, shared them not only on military campaigns, but also on our travels and vacations in the countryside.

104. Why should I even mention our passions for knowledge and learning, on which, away from the eyes of the crowd, we spent all our leisure? If the recollections and memories of such things had died with him, I wouldn't be able to bear the loss of a man so near and dear

modo possem; sed nec illa exstincta sunt, alun-
turque potius et augentur cogitatione et memo-
ria mea. Et si illis plane orbatus essem, magnum
tamen adfert mihi aetas ipsa solacium; diutius
enim iam in hoc desiderio esse non possum;
omnia autem brevia tolerabilia esse debent,
etiamsi magna sunt.

Haec habui de amicitia quae dicerem; vos
autem hortor ut ita virtutem locetis, sine qua
amicitia esse non potest, ut ea excepta nihil
amicitia praestabilius putetis.

to me. But these experiences are not dead. To the contrary, as I reflect on and remember our time together, the memories are nourished and strengthened. Even if someday I am deprived of the ability to remember Scipio, my age itself provides some comfort, for I won't have to miss him much longer. We should be able to endure any pain that is brief, no matter how terrible.

That is all I have to say about friendship. As for you, my young friends, I urge you to strive for virtue, for without it friendship cannot exist. And friendship, aside from virtue, is the greatest thing we can find in life.

NOTES

Latin text by permission of Oxford University Press. © Oxford University Press. M. Tullius Cicero, *De Re Publica, De Legibus, Cato Maior de Senectutue, Laelius de Amicitia*, edited by J. G. F. Powell. Oxford: Oxford University Press, 2006.

1. Quintus Mucius Scaevola, an eminent lawyer, was consul in 117 BC.
2. An augur was a member of an official guild of diviners who, among other duties, observed the sky for omens.
3. Gaius Laelius, consul in 140 BC, was a celebrated orator and patron of Greek philosophers, earning him the nickname *Sapiens* ("the wise").
4. A young Roman man put on the *toga virilis* ("toga of manhood") at sixteen or seventeen.
5. This Quintus Mucius Scaevola, a distinguished lawyer, was consul in 95 BC.

6. The pontifex maximus was the chief priest of the Roman state.

7. Titus Pomponius Atticus (110–32 BC), the best friend of Cicero from boyhood.

8. Publius Sulpicius Rufus sided with Marius in his armed conflict with Sulla, whereas Quintus Pompeius Rufus, consul in 88 BC, sided with Sulla.

9. The tribunes of the plebs were magistrates whose formal duty was to defend the rights of the people.

10. Rome had two consuls elected each year who were the leading magistrates of the state.

11. Gaius Fannius, consul in 122 BC.

12. Publius Cornelius Scipio Aemilianus Africanus defeated the Carthaginians in the Third Punic War, but died under mysterious circumstances.

13. Marcus Porcius Cato (235–149 BC) was a prominent Roman politician and orator who was celebrated for his old-fashioned virtues. The book Cicero refers to is known as *Cato Maior* or *De Senectute*, which I have translated as part of this

series under the title *How to Grow Old* (Princeton, 2016).

14. Literally, his *cognomen*, the final name for a Roman male, often inherited, but given to individuals in special cases for distinguished service in government or war.

15. The Seven Sages were Greeks traditionally judged to be the wisest of their people. The list varies somewhat, but generally includes Solon of Athens, Thales of Miletus, Pittacus of Mytilene, Bias of Priene, Cleobus of Rhodes, Myson of Chenae, and Chilon of Sparta. The man declared most wise by the oracle of Apollo at Delphi was Socrates.

16. The augurs met on the Nones of each month (the fifth or seventh day). Decimus Brutus was consul in 138 BC.

17. Lucius Aemilius Paulus was a celebrated general who served as consul in 182 and 168 BC. Gaius Sulpicius Galus was consul in 166 BC.

18. Carthage (146 BC) and Numantia in Spain (133 BC).

19. The day before his death, Scipio had fought with his political enemy Carbo in the Senate over an agrarian law. The next day he was found dead in his bed, with many suspecting it was Carbo who had him killed.

20. The followers of the Greek philosopher Pythagoras who taught reincarnation.

21. Scipio Africanus the Elder, who defeated Hannibal at the Battle of Zama in 202 BC, was consul in 204 and 194 BC. Cicero relates this imagined three-day discussion with the *Dream of Scipio* in his book *On the State*.

22. Theseus and Pirithous, Achilles and Patroclus, Orestes and Pylades, Damon and Phintias (Pythias).

23. Gaius Fabricius Luscanius (consul in 282 and 278 BC) refused bribes from the invading general Pyrrhus; Manius Curius Dentatus (consul in 290, 275, and 274 BC) defeated Pyrrhus; Tiberius Coruncanius (consul in 280 BC) was a successful general and the first plebian to serve as pontifex maximus, the chief priest of Rome.

24. Ennius (239–169 BC) was an early Roman poet much admired by Cicero.

25. The Greek philosopher Empedocles lived on the island of Sicily in the fifth century BC.

26. Pacuvius was a south Italian dramatist who lived in the second century BC before Cicero was born. In the incident referred to here, the friends Pylades and Orestes are captured by natives of the Crimea and are sentenced to death for trying to steal an image of the goddess Artemis.

27. Tradition says Tarquin, who ruled from 534 to 509 BC, was the last king of Rome. Spurius Cassius Vecellinus and Spurius Maelius in the fifth century were accused of attempting to overthrow the republic and return Rome to monarchy. Pyrrhus of Epirus in western Greece invaded Italy in 280 BC, while the Carthaginian general Hannibal crossed the Alps into Italy in 218 BC and threatened the destruction of the Rome.

28. The Roman aristocrat Gnaeus Marcius Coriolanus conspired with Rome's neighbors to take over the city in the early fifth century BC.

29. Tiberius Sempronius Gracchus attempted radical reform the Republic through land reform and other measures, but was killed by a gang of senators in 133 BC. Glaius Blossius was a Stoic philosopher who later committed suicide in Asia after he rebelled against the Romans and was defeated.

30. Gaius Papirius Carbo was tribune probably in 130 BC, while Gaius Porius Cato became consul in 114 BC.

31. The Gabinian Law of 139 BC introduced voting by secret ballot. The Cassian Law two years later extended the vote by ballot to juries in criminal cases.

32. Themistocles abandoned Athens around 471 BC. Other ancient sources say both Coriolanus and Themistocles lived long lives and died natural deaths in exile.

33. This is a very difficult paragraph to translate as it's not clear exactly what Cicero is trying to say and because he seems to contradict the noble view of duty within friendship he advocates earlier.

34. Lucius Furius Philus (consul 136 BC); Publius Rupilius (consul 132 BC); Lucius Mummius (consul 146 BC); Quintus Fabius Maximus Aemilianus (consul 145 BC).

35. Quintus Pompeius Rufus defeated Laelius and became consul in 141 BC by allegedly pretending at first not to be a candidate. Quintus Caecilius Metellus Macedonicus (consul 143 BC) was, at the time this dialogue is set, a colleague of Laelius in the College of Augurs.

36. A figure who may have lived in the fifth-century BC. He is first mentioned by Aristophanes and became the subject of Shakespeare's play.

37. Archytas of Tarentum in southern Italy was a Greek philosopher and scientist of the fourth century BC.

38. *Andrian Girl* (*Andria*) 69. Terence lived in the second century BC.

39. *Eunuch* 250.

40. 130 BC.

41. 145 BC.

42. Terence *Eunuch* 391.

43. From Caecilius Statius *Heiress*.

44. Lucius Aemilius Paullus (consul 182 and 168 BC), Marcus Porcius Cato (consul 195 BC), Gaius Sulpicius Galus (consul 166 BC), Publius Cornelius Scipio Nasica (consul 191 BC), and Tiberius Gracchus (consul 177), father of the reform-minded Gracchi brothers.

45. Lucius Furius Philo (consul 136 BC), Publius Rupilius (consul 132 BC), Spurius Mummius (consul 146 BC), and Publius Rutilius (consul 105 BC). Aulus Verginius is otherwise unknown.

FURTHER READING

Cicero, Marcus Tullius. *How to Grow Old: Ancient Wisdom for the Second Half of Life*. Translated and with an introduction by Philip Freeman. Princeton: Princeton University Press, 2016.

——. *How to Run a Country: An Ancient Guide for Modern Leaders*. Selected, translated, and with an introduction by Philip Freeman. Princeton: Princeton University Press, 2013.

——. *On the Good Life*. Translated with an introduction by Michael Grant. New York: Penguin Books, 1971.

Cicero, Quintus Tullius. *How to Win an Election: An Ancient Guide for Modern Politicians*.

Translated with an introduction by Philip Freeman. Princeton: Princeton University Press, 2012.

Everitt, Anthony. *Cicero: The Life and Times of Rome's Greatest Politician*. New York: Random House, 2001.

Gruen, Erich. *The Last Generation of the Roman Republic*. Berkeley: University of California Press, 1995.

Rawson, Elizabeth. *Cicero: A Portrait*. London: Bristol Classical Press, 1983.

Richard, Carl J. *The Founders and the Classics: Greece, Rome, and the American Enlightenment*. Cambridge: Harvard University Press, 1994.

Scullard, H. H. *From the Gracchi to Nero: A History of Rome from 133 BC to AD 68*. New York: Routledge, 1982.

Syme, Ronald. *The Roman Revolution*. Oxford: Oxford University Press, 2002.